TELEVISION STUDIES

Sue & Wink Hackman

HODDER AND STOUGHTON
LONDON SYDNEY AUCKLAND TORONTO

Acknowledgments

The authors and publishers would like to thank the following for their permission to reproduce material in this book:

Picador for Clive James: *The Crystal Bucket* (p. 101); *The Observer* for their television listings (p. 86); William Heinemann Ltd and Aitken and Stones for Alison Lurie: *The War Between the Tates* (pp. 75 and 78); *Spare Rib* for a review from the July 1978 issue (p. 102); *Hounslow Star* for television listings from the 19 May 1987 issue (p. 85); Marvel Comics Group for *Dr Who Weekly* 28 May 1980 (pp. 57–8); BBC Publications for television listings (p. 86) and photographs (pp. 13 and 93); BARB/AGB for viewing statistics for the week ending 15 March 1987 which are reprinted by permission (pp. 14 and 26); London Weekend Television for photographs (pp. 26, 33, 50, 70, 93, 27 – by permission of Bruce Forsyth, 29 – by permission of Cilla Black, 64–5 – by permission of Michael Brandon and Glynis Barber); ORACLE for reviews (p. 105).

Cover pictures kindly supplied by Spectrum (top right), Ace Photo Agency (top left, middle and bottom left) and Scottish Television (bottom right).

British Cataloguing in Publication Data
Hackman, Sue
  Television studies.
  1. Television – For media studies Students
  I. Title   II. Hackman, Wink
  621.388
  ISBN 0 340 42520 2

First published 1988

Typeset in Linotron Electra by Rowland Phototypesetting Limited, Bury St Edmunds, Suffolk. Printed in Great Britain for Hodder and Stoughton Educational, a division of Hodder and Stoughton Limited, Mill Road, Dunton Green, Sevenoaks, Kent by Butler & Tanner Limited, Frome, Somerset

Contents

Note to the Teacher

This book has arisen out of our joint experience of classroom teaching and broadcast television. Believing that current programmes are the ideal resources for television studies, we have avoided linking the activities to specific programmes, so that the teacher can select material which is topical, available and appropriate.

Teachers who have access to video equipment will be relieved to learn that all the practical exercises can be recorded using one camera, and that editing is not necessary. Teachers who enjoy the luxury of several cameras and editing facilities will find the material easy to adapt.

Teachers who are venturing into practical video work for the first time might start with the practical assignment in the section entitled *Reading Television*, where some of the unwritten rules of camera work are explored. In general, however, we have aimed to give a greater degree of initiative to students in the later exercises. Be warned that practical video work always takes three times longer than you expect.

We think that most of the work would be best accomplished in small groups. We notice that this is the method students use to discuss television in students' own time. It is a secure environment for soliciting and sharing opinions, and for venturing into the more demanding practical activities.

Teachers should realise that students already conduct their own extra-curricular television studies with enthusiasm. Respect their expertise and build on it. It is almost a reflex action of teachers to treat television as a debased cultural phenomenon, and to see their teaching as a corrective. Alas, students will soon find you out if you lack an open mind. It is not our intention to preach a better culture to your students, but to locate them where they can arrive at informed judgements for themselves.

Finally, we wish to record our thanks to London Weekend Television and their employees who have been generous with their time and help.

Sue and Wink Hackman

Permission is granted to photocopy pages 42–3, 64–5, 72–3 and 82–3 for class use only.

PART ONE / *Popular Genres*

In this part of the book we look at examples of different types of television programme. 'Genre' is a word you probably haven't used before but it just means a particular type or sort of programme, such as a game show, a soap opera or a situation comedy. *Coronation Street*, *EastEnders*, *Dallas* and *Dynasty* are all examples from the genre of soap operas.

We come to know the different genres very well and we know what to expect from them in terms of their story and style. The way we watch a particular programme is affected by the genre we place it in. If we expect a programme to be a documentary, for example, we would be surprised to hear the commentator crack a joke. Equally, we would be taken aback if our favourite comedian appeared in a serious role – say, announcing the news. We would be constantly waiting for the punchline.

Many of these genres originated before the start of television, in film, radio and theatre. The game show *Give Us A Clue* is clearly inspired by the parlour game of charades, and several situation comedies bring to mind the theatre tradition of farce.

Television programmes are made by teams of people – actors, script writers, designers, directors and so on – and each section focuses on the vital role of these people working behind the scenes. They are the people whose names you see in the credits at the end of the programme, but rarely pause to consider.

Detectives

INTRODUCTION

First of all, make a list of all the television detective programmes you can remember.

e.g. *Dempsey and Makepeace*
Magnum

Now, fill in a table like this for each of them:

	Example
Name	Dempsey and Makepeace
Age	20s/30s
Appearance	She: smart, fashionable He: casual
Relationship to police	Special squad
Relationships with superiors	Uneasy. Superiors seen as old-fashioned and slow. Mutual distrust.
Personal relationships	Love/hate relationship. Possible romance?
Style of work	Quick. Aggressive. Usually ends in brawl or shoot-out.
Unusual features	Contrasts: He is American, streetwise She is English, upper-class
How he/she speaks	He: New York street accent She: Posh upper-class English

After completing work on a number of detectives, do you see any common features? For example, it is often the case that TV detectives work in special secret units and their relationship with their superiors is poor. This makes them appealing to the viewer after a hard day being bossed around at school or work. We too want to feel more powerful and special. It also gives the writer more opportunities to introduce exciting under-cover jobs – the sort which are, in reality, rather rare.

Look over your examples and spot any other common features, and explain why they might appeal to the viewer as well as being useful to the writer.

CREATING A CHARACTER

It takes planning and teamwork to create a character:

The character who appears on the screen is the end-result of a team effort which involves all these people. Changes and compromises have to be made.

TRY IT YOURSELF

Imagine you are one of the team launching a new television detective series. You have the following outline of the character:

Name: Maggie Rose

Age: 40s

Background: very poor childhood
                     a hard life on the streets
                     lives alone – no relatives

Personality: clever
                     blunt
                     independent
                     occasional dry humour
                     has no time for her superior officers, whom she sees as slow-witted
                     and blundering

First of all, you must help with the *casting* – choosing which actor should play the part. You have a shortlist of four actors to choose from:

1 Helen Thompson   Helen Thompson is already a household name for a character she plays in the hit soap opera *Southenders*. She is famous, popular and experienced. However, the public associates her with this other character – can she make the change? She will be expensive to employ.

2 Vera Faraday   Vera Faraday is an unknown actor with little experience, but she performed very well at the audition. She will be inexpensive to employ, but is rather young for the part and inexperienced – will she be up to the job?

3 Lesley Jones   Lesley Jones has a distinguished career in film and theatre. She is considered to be one of the most talented actors on stage today. However, she has no television experience, and this is not the kind of role she is used to playing. She is a fine actor – she has played many big parts in Shakespeare's plays, for example – but can she make the transition into popular television?

4 Stella Parsons   Stella Parsons is an experienced television actor. She is known as a pleasant, able and reliable sort. She hasn't had a really big part yet, but this one would suit her. You are sure she could play the part, but perhaps she lacks sparkle. Will she rise to the challenge?

Make a list of all the things you should bear in mind in choosing the actor for the part. In a group, exchange notes and discuss which person you would employ.

Helen Thompson

Vera Faraday

Lesley Jones

Stella Parsons

Now prepare a portfolio of information, sketches and speeches which will help your chosen actor to become the character Maggie Rose:

The **costume** designer will prepare a sketch of her in typical clothes.

The **make-up** artist will draw her portrait, with an appropriate hairstyle and make-up.

The **scriptwriter** will prepare two or three typical speeches to illustrate her personality:

(a) a telephone conversation with an anxious client or informer
(b) bursting into the classroom to arrest a highly dangerous teacher
(c) being told off in the boss's office

Supporting information   Other members of the team will help to prepare the chosen actor by thinking up more details about her lifestyle and habits. They might make sketches of her living room, imagine what she likes to eat, what car she likes to drive, and so on.

PRACTICAL ASSIGNMENT

This assignment is to rehearse some scenes from *Maggie Rose*, based on the scripted examples you wrote in the last exercise. You will need:

    a camera operator
    a director (to organise and take decisions)
    Maggie Rose
    the boss
    the teacher
    students

Some people are camera-shy and it is usually they who end up behind the camera or hanging around. Try not to let this happen, for these good reasons:

- everyone should have a go at the camera, at directing, and at acting
- you will learn more from being involved
- it will help your confidence to try it now, in class, where the group will be sympathetic
- nervousness is a normal part of acting in public
- you are asked to perform because you can learn something from it which you can't learn from reading or from watching other people

1   Try the **telephone scene** first, because you can do this with one camera and no cuts. Set up the camera to include Maggie and the telephone, and when the actor has had a chance to rehearse, just record it in one take.

2   Next rehearse the scene **bursting into the classroom**. Record it in two shots. First, a shot of Maggie taken from behind, heading for the classroom and opening the door.

Just as she opens the door, stop the tape and take the camera into the classroom. Put it where it can see the class, the teacher and the door. You will need quick timing to catch Maggie just as she enters and shouts 'Freeze!' or whatever. Keep the camera running long enough to capture the reaction of the class. Use more shots if you want to continue beyond this – for example, a close-up of the teacher's reaction.

3 The **office scene** is more difficult. Start it this way:

/ A first shot outside the office shows Maggie knocking at the boss's door . . .

/ A second shot inside the office shows the boss at a desk and a door in the background through which Maggie will enter . . .

/ A closer shot of the boss now . . .

/ A new, medium range shot of the desk as Maggie takes a seat and the interview begins . . .

/ This fourth shot will do for the rest of the interview unless you wish to experiment with close-ups and Maggie's exit.

Afterwards . . .

Compare results and discuss the difficulties you encountered in this exercise. The following checklist may be useful:

- immediate reactions
- the experience of seeing yourself on screen
- the experience of acting on video
- technical aspects – sound, lighting, camerawork, etc.
- moments that 'feel wrong' – why?
- successful moments

After the practical assignment, you will find it useful to watch similar scenes on broadcast television to see how professionals tackle them.

VIEWING ASSIGNMENT

In the next week, try to watch a few minutes from an episode of a detective series. Jot down your impressions of the detective's character and how it is conveyed. Notice, for example, the hairstyle, the clothes, the speech, the lifestyle and so on. Afterwards, write a brief report of your findings.

Soap Operas

INTRODUCTION

Soap operas are serials such as *EastEnders* and *Dallas* which feature regular characters and never-ending stories. If you watch them, you already know what complicated and dramatic lives the characters in soap operas seem to lead!

These programmes are called **soap operas** because the first ones were financed on American television by companies who made soap and detergents. The many people who tuned in to watch each exciting episode also sat through the soap advertisements which appeared during it. It was an advertising ploy.

Get together in groups and make a list of all the soap operas you know:

e.g.   *EastEnders*
        Dallas

Discuss which ones you watch, if any, and which ones you prefer. Consider, also, particular characters and incidents which interest or irritate you.

/ *Familiar faces from* EastEnders

Soap operas attract massive audiences. These are the viewing figures (in millions) for the week ending 15 March 1987:

EastEnders	24.6	*Dynasty*	9.8
Coronation Street	16.4	*Brookside*	6.5
Dallas	11.3	*Falcon Crest*	5.1
Emmerdale Farm	10.8		

(Reprinted by permission of BARB/AGB. The audiences to *Eastenders* are the aggregation of the original transmissions on Tuesday and Thursday with the audiences for the repeat on Sundays. Individuals who watched the programme twice are not eliminated.)

Unlike most television stories, the plot of a soap opera never ends. The story goes on and on and on for as long as people continue to tune in. In a sense, soap operas are close to our own lives, which also continue to unfold. Although the characters live lives completely removed from ours, in places we never visit, we may find in their everyday emotions a reflection of our own. They have intense relationships and powerful moments of emotion, and however exaggerated and frequent these are, we recognise them and perhaps yearn to live our own lives at that more exciting pitch.

PLOT

Soap operas are often based on the fortunes of one huge family or tightly-knit communities such as these:

/ A *map of* Dynasty *characters by student* **Vicki Edwards**

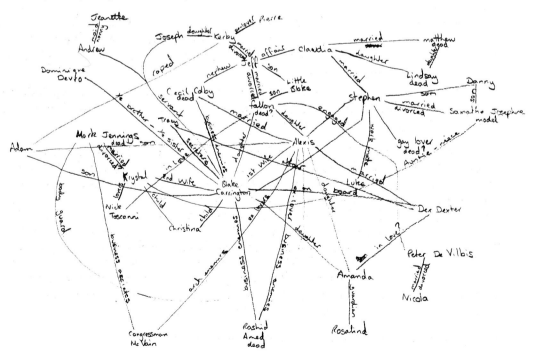

/ A *map of* Coronation Street *relationships by student* **J. Payne**

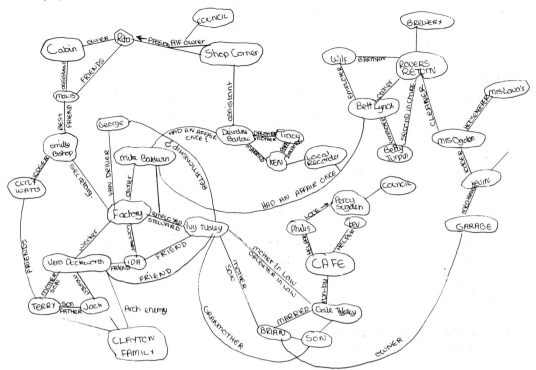

Why do writers find huge families and tightly-knit communities useful as the setting for their plots?

The team who writes the soap opera will plan months ahead what will happen in the plot – who will marry, who will have problems, who will fall in love. New characters may be introduced and old ones leave. This can be tricky. Think of examples, and discuss how such changes are managed.

Next, the writers will prepare a **storyline** (an outline of the plot) for each episode and then someone goes away to write a script for the actors. This is the **storyline** for one episode of an imaginary soap opera:

Jennifer has discovered that Sandra is her long-lost sister, and rushes round to The Ranch to reveal the truth. Sandra does not believe the news and orders Jennifer to leave. Meanwhile, Mr Beadle has told his partner that he intends to quit the business when he reaches his sixtieth birthday, at which time his daughter Barbara will take over. This alarms his partner, Slim Tucker, who hates young Barbara Beadle since she refused to marry him last year. He starts to plan ways of keeping the business to himself. Jennifer flies to Spain to see her mother, now married to Mr Beadle's wicked brother, Raymond. She begs her mother to persuade Sandra that she really is her sister, but after asking for a few days to think it over, her mother makes a hushed and secretive phone call to a mysterious person: 'She's fallen for it!' Jennifer, enjoying the unexpected sunshine, notices the attentions of a handsome guest at the same hotel . . .

The **script writer** is left to work out the details and the dialogue.

TRY IT YOURSELF

Use the storyline given above to draw a diagram showing the network of relationships on which this soap opera is based.

Draw sketches of the four or five main characters and write a brief description of each personality as you imagine it.

Write a storyline for the next episode.

Choose one brief scene between two or three of the characters and write a detailed script.

PRACTICAL ASSIGNMENT

Make a video of the scene you have just scripted.

- Prepare an acting area.
- Go through the script and break it down into short sections. The purpose of these sections is to give the camera operator an opportunity to move position, and also to make it easier for the actors to remember their parts.
- Appoint a camera operator, actors and a director to organise people and take decisions.
- Rehearse each section and then record it. If you are not satisfied, record over it.

Afterwards . . .

Watch your video and discuss its merits and its shortcomings. Write a report for the teacher describing your own part in the assignment, your reactions to the experience, and say how you rate the video.

VIEWING ASSIGNMENT

Watch one episode of a popular soap opera, keeping a note of the scenes as they happen. Prepare an account of the episode (no more than 200 words) and draw a diagram to show the relationships of the characters to each other. Then consider these questions:

- What do you think will happen next?
- What comments, incidents or clues made you think this?
- How do the writers encourage the audience to tune in for the next episode?

These are important questions for the writers of soap operas, because winning bigger audiences depends on being able to hook the attention of new viewers even in the middle of the story. They must build in situations which will tempt the curiosity of the audience and make them watch on to find out what happens next . . .

Comedy

INTRODUCTION

Comedy is perhaps the most popular form of television programme. It is not really surprising, since all of us crack jokes at home, at school or college, in everyday life. Even tiny babies laugh; it is a natural human reflex. And we laugh at a wide range of things: a mishap, an embarrassment, a play on words, someone in a fix, an unexpected or misplaced object, an impersonation. The laughter itself can be bitter, or perhaps nervous or even an uncontrollable belly laugh. Comedy is the oldest and widest-ranging of the genres we see on television.

We are used to seeing comic programmes which are fast-moving and fun-packed. Television comedy is written and edited to be quickfire, and feels rather different from live comedy. Writing comic scripts for television is complex because the writer has to see as well as hear the joke as it will be on the screen. Cut off from the audience at home, the writer has to be sure that the material will 'work', since there are no second chances.

WRITING A SCRIPT

The comedians Hale and Pace, perhaps better known to you as Ron and Ron the Eastend gangsters, wrote the script for their own TV series *The Management*, as well as comic sketches for programmes such as *Saturday Gang* and *Saturday Live*. **Norman Pace** explains how they work on a script:

How do you go about writing a script for television?
We start by mapping out the plot in scene order to give an outline. We try to write lots of short scenes that keep the audience's attention throughout – no more than about two minutes each. You're writing for the end of the scene all the time – you know where it's going and you're looking for a visual or verbal punchline. Then we really just argue about every line – I might say 'What can this character say here?' and we both start to put on voices and talk the way the character would, and experiment until we feel we've got the best from it. Once the characters are firm in the mind, they start to take on a life of their own. Our scripts aren't particularly scribbly because we've usually decided what we want to say before we write anything.

How does writing for television differ from writing a sketch for the stage?
Writing sketches for television is brilliant because you can just cut from the last joke to the next sketch. In live theatre you have to end every sketch on a high note or you walk off to the audience groaning. So television sketch shows can make it easier on the writer. But when you write situation comedy it's quite different – the plot is the most important

/ *Gareth Hale and Norman Pace as Ron and Ron*

thing. There's no hiding place in sitcom – if the plot doesn't make sense, the audience feels let down.

What constraints does television impose on the writer?
Obviously money is an enormous constraint – I'd love to write as Kenny Everett did – 'I drive a Chieftain tank through the wall'. Very simple and it gets a big laugh – but it's just the cost that stops you from doing that very often. Television producers also want to play safe. They don't want to take risks with new ideas and so controversial programmes do get ditched.

Some sketches which are funny in the theatre don't come over well on television. I remember one of the best things we've done live was a parody of the Queen song 'Bohemian Rhapsody' featuring five people playing dustbin lids, spoons and bits of crockery. We sing the whole thing, including the middle bit that not even Queen do. Audiences go mad when they see it on stage but on the screen it just doesn't work. The director has to choose between a wide shot, where you look like ants, or close-ups which miss out what's going on. You have to write to take advantage of the close-up. That's what television comedy is all about – showing close-ups of facial expressions, seeing the comedian's eyes.

You have to listen to other people's opinions as well and alter scenes in the light of criticism. That's hard at the time, but it often improves the end result. For example, we

N/. A word in your shell like. We

G/ The management

N/ Have noticed that certain elements of you

G/ The audience

N/ Have been smirking It's a shame that. That is a shame. Because 'as Ron always says

G/ Smirking .. can seriously damage your health.

N/. O dear Ron ... They're laughing now .... Tut x5

G/ And one from me   TUT.

N/ L+G Don't laugh at Ron cos it makes him feel stupid

G/ Stupid Ron

N/. So don't laugh no more

G/. Moron.

N/ Business. Ron and I have decided to disembark on a new business venture. We have noticed lackadaisy how unfit you have become   so we have opened a new gymnasium called ... ..

G/ Gym's Ron ..... Ron's gym.

N/. The gym has all modern conveniences

G/. And toilets ───→ N/ For the ladies G/ Heavy robies N/. In the form of shape up and dance with Ron G/ Or else

N/. It is ideal for all forms of training.

G/ Fitness training, circuit training and ...... weight training.

N/. Or why not relax in our B posh bath full of bubble and waves and that, a jaccousteau. Or if you're a little chubby why not lose weight quickly in Ron's special sauna In the gym Ron here helped If you're a little chubby fear not Just last week a a lady managed to lose two stone in an afternoon. How'd you manage that Ron

G/ Sauna

N/ Sauna Ron ?

G/ Yeah I sauna leg off.

N/. Halves the price of footwear. A word of advice join our very expensive club now, or you're health might go down hill very rapidly when Ron pays you a visit and gets out his do dah.

G/ The do dah Ron   N/ or The do dah Ron

/ A draft script for a Ron and Ron sketch

wrote a scene in *The Management* in which one of the Rons takes on Fat Charlie in a snooker match. Neither of them can play so they each get a champion to play for them. We showed it to the producer and other people and they said, 'It's just not funny enough – snooker's been done before, it's old hat'. We had to admit they were right, and so we completely rewrote the scene as a whelk-eating contest – and it made it much more original.

Do you think comedy is changing?
Yes, it has to. The tradition of the northern club circuit and the end-of-pier show – all that's waning now. Television has taken over; it's slick and fast-moving, and the old stuff won't do any longer. Audiences expect the pace and visual interest that television can give. Sitcom is a very staid, traditional format – you have to crack through that to produce something fresh, in the way that *The Young Ones* did. We hope *The Management* will do so too.

Norman Pace, writer and actor, *The Management*

TRY IT YOURSELF

Produce a short script for a comic video sketch based on *one* of the following ideas from Hale and Pace, whose own drafts are shown at various stages of completion on the following pages. The script might go through several stages before it is ready for the cameras.

1 *The Addict* A sketch in which a person confesses an innocent but bizarre addiction.
   Hale and Pace prepared a script about a sand addict who later became hooked on boulders. Opposite are their very first notes, jotted down as the ideas came.

2 *Soap* A three-minute version of a familiar soap opera which features all the main characters and summarises all the typical plots.
   This is Hale and Pace's first draft for a three-minute *Dallas*:

The Three-Minute Dallas

JR   Hello. My name's JR. I'm a nasty piece of work. Here I am having b'fast by my luxurious swimming pool.
S/E   Hello, I'm Sue Ellen. I used to have a drink problem but I'm all right now. I'm going to buy some clothes now. Time for you to go to the office, JR.
JR   OK, bye.
S/E   Bye. (*Exit*)

Enter Clayton

CLAYTON   Hello, I'm Clayton Farlow. I'm married to Miss Ellie. I'm worried because there's something different about her.

① Intro — Man on the Run — shock — John
  Let's talk about the early days what are your first
② Infant school → sandpit — tried it → liked it *late some memories*

② Did you find your visits to the pit became more
  regular?

  Yeah sports day → hJ + LJ raking anything
  to be near it yknow. But it didn't stop there

③ It led on to harder ~~stuff~~ stuff?

  Yeah.... gravel .... I remember in
  Bob a Job week. walking up someones
  driveway. took handful went home

④ How did you take it?
  Tried Smoking ... kept falling off snuffing it →
  so well swallowed it

⑤ Did you ever inject it?
  No — I know a bloke who did —
  lumpy arm .. from gravel? — Pebbledashed his house
⑥ Any side effects from gravel? — did it?
⑦ But it didn't stop there did it?

  No — 17 — scooters, Brighton → on beach
  pebbles, boulders rocky outcrops we just got stoned didn't
  one meaning mates took 3 levels of a multi storey car park
  care, and then I got pulled by the old bill
  and arrested by the police.

⑧ You were sent to prison?
  yeah — with 3 days I ate my way out.

⑨ Are you still on the stuff
  No I've Kicked it, broke 2 toes.
  I've

⑩ .

/ 'The Addict' – Hale and Pace's first draft

MISS ELLIE	Hello, I'm the new Miss Ellie. I love you Clayton but I love my boys as well. Bye.
LUCY	Hello, I'm Lucy. I'm short and spoilt, but I've only got a small part. Bye.
CLAYTON	Meanwhile, back in JR's office . . . Bye.
JR	Here I am in my office about to do an evil deed. Ha ha ha. (*Phone*) Hello, this is JR.
CLIFF	Hello, this is Cliff Barnes, an ambitious business man.
JR	I hate you.
CLIFF	I hate you too.
JR	Bye.
CLIFF	Bye.
JR	Meanwhile back at the ranch . . .
RAY	EastEnders are coming!

Enter Bobby and Pam

BOBBY	Hello, I'm Bobby. I'm attractive and good. Most of the time, I'm miserable.
PAM	Hello, I'm Pam. I'm attractive and good as well. Most of the time, I'm crying.
BOBBY	I wear lots of hairspray.
PAM	I wear lots of lip gloss.
RAY	I'm Ray. I'm a cowboy.
BOBBY	Pam, will you marry me?
PAM	Yes I will.
BOBBY	Pam, will you divorce me?
PAM	Yes I will.
BOBBY	Pam, will you remarry me in a future episode?
PAM	I wouldn't be surprised, but I still love Mark Grayson.

Enter Mark

MARK	Hello, I'm Mark Grayson. I die in a plane crash. (*Throws paper plane.*) Argh! Bye.
BOBBY AND PAM	Bye.
JR	Hello. I'm JR, just home from an evil day's work at the office. I get the sneaky feeling somebody's going to shoot me.
ALL	You're right . . . 1-2-3-BANG!
JR	I think I'm dead.
ALL	And we all lived happily ever after. Bye bye.

3 *The New Act*   A sketch in which comedians try to get their agent to take on an improbable new act.

Hale and Pace wrote a script about an Invisible Act. In this later draft, stage directions are included. The writing takes into account what the sketch will look like on the screen, and how props will be used. Notice how the last joke depends on the use of video recording and editing – it could not easily be achieved live.

The Invisible Brothers

Office interior. The MANAGER *is in his office. The intercom rings.*

MANAGER	Yes, Janice?
JANICE	It's Hale and Pace to see you with their new act.
MANAGER	What is it this time?
JANICE	The Amazing Invisible Brothers.
MANAGER	All right, send them in.

The door swings open. Nothing happens for five seconds. GARETH *and* NORMAN *sneak in trying to look invisible.* GARETH *stands in front of the filing cabinet,* NORMAN *stands in front of the fireplace.*

GARETH	We are the Invisible Brothers. I am Gareth Invisible.
NORMAN	And I am Norman Invisible.
GARETH AND NORMAN	We are totally and completely invisible.

Meanwhile, the MANAGER *has been busying himself with paperwork completely ignoring* GARETH *and* NORMAN. *He looks up.*

MANAGER	Hello, Gareth. Hello, Norman.
GARETH	What invisible force makes this tea cup float through the air?

GARETH *carries cup through air.* NORMAN *plays Swanee whistle for effects.*

NORMAN	What invisible power mysteriously brings the curtains to life?

NORMAN *rustles curtains.* GARETH *plays whistle.*

GARETH	What unseen source of energy lifts a waste paper basket?

GARETH *lifts waste paper basket,* NORMAN *plays whistle.*

NORMAN	What invisible force can hurl this filing cabinet across the room and through the window?

NORMAN *fights to lift filing cabinet.* GARETH *is playing the whistle.*

MANAGER	No, no, hang on. That's enough.
GARETH AND NORMAN	What?
MANAGER	That's enough. Now get out.
GARETH AND NORMAN	But you can't see us, we're The Invisible Brothers.
MANAGER	Gareth, I can see you there. Norman, I can see you there. Now get out.
GARETH AND NORMAN	But . . .
MANAGER	Get out.
GARETH AND NORMAN	But . . .
MANAGER	Get out . . . get out of my sight.
GARETH AND NORMAN	OK.

They play their Swanee whistles and they completely vanish.

PRACTICAL ASSIGNMENT

In the same group, prepare to record two comic video sketches: the Bench Sketch, which is silent, and the Hale and Pace sketch you scripted earlier.

1 Bench Sketch

Set up a video camera opposite a bench, and rehearse the following scene:

A sits close to the end of the bench.

B arrives and sits at the end. **A** is obliged to shuffle along a little.

C arrives, begs pardon and asks **A** to move along so that he can sit between them.

D arrives, spots friend **C** and sits down to chatter between **B** and **C**. **A** has to move along to the end of the bench.

E arrives and so on . . .

Finally, **A** falls off the end of the bench, brushes off the dust, begs **C**'s pardon and tries to get a space created as the others have done. He is refused.

As he fumes and complains, **B** gets up and goes, but a new person arrives and takes the vacant space just before **A** gets to it.

You can continue this scene indefinitely. How will it end? Work out some clever way for **A** to get a seat, or to get revenge. Do it without dialogue, like a silent movie.

You should find this easy to record, because the one camera can be fixed and the recorder left to run. If you do it this way, the actors will need to exaggerate their reactions because the camera cannot see the details of their facial expressions, and being silent there are no verbal clues. However, if you feel confident, you may try including close-ups and zooms which will catch the faces of the actors – but you may need to stop and start to allow the camera operator time to move into position. In this case, actors will have to remember exactly how they are placed when the cut comes – small changes are easily noticed.

2 Prepared Script

Using the script you prepared in the earlier exercise, appoint actors, a director and a camera operator to record it on video.

During rehearsal, decide which moments, if any, should be in close-up so that the action can stop to allow the camera operator to change the shot. Rehearse again for the sake of the camera operator, so that he or she can check that there is a good view from the new position. Check your progress as you go along, so that corrections can be made on the spot. This is easier than trying to record over a section later, when the split-second timing can be lost.

Afterwards . . .

Play back your recording and pay close attention firstly to the timing or pace of the pieces, and secondly to the use of close-ups. Why are these two aspects so important in television comedy?

VIEWING ASSIGNMENT

Watch out for comedians at work in different programmes on television this week. Try to find:

- a comedian hosting a game show
- a comedian starring in a situation comedy
- a guest comedian on someone else's show
- comedians working as a pair

Study each one for two or three minutes. Do you notice any differences in the type of humour they use, the style of the delivery and the butt of the jokes – and can you account for these differences? Jot down the details and think about the questions so that you are ready to discuss them later.

Game Shows

INTRODUCTION

The great popularity of game shows is illustrated by the viewing figures (in millions) for the week ending 15 March 1987:

Blankety Blank	14.0	*Sporting Triangles*	10.9
Bob's Full House	12.8	*Catchphrase*	10.9
Question of Sport	11.8	*The Price is Right*	10.0

(Reprinted by permission of BARB/AGB.)

Many programmes involve members of the public as contestants, for example in documentaries and street interviews. But overall, guests have a minor role and are carefully guided through the performance by an interviewer or host. The game show is no exception; notice the way contestants are guided on and off the set by assistants, and the way they are directed by the host. Indeed, it is part of the host's job to organise them, as the name 'host' implies. Remember how participants are often stationed in one particular place whilst the host moves around, and you will see that their involvement is strictly limited.

/ *The studio audience watching* Play Your Cards Right

/ *Bruce Forsyth hosting* Play Your Cards Right

THE HOST

Make a list of all the game shows you have seen. Next to each one, write the name of the *host*.

SHOW	HOST	IMAGE
Mastermind	Magnus Magnusson	Serious, intellectual
Blind Date	Cilla Black	Girl-next-door type

Each host has an image to keep up. Jot down one or two words next to each host to describe his or her image. You may be able to name their distinctive features such as catchphrases, appearance or their brand of humour. These are their trademarks, and an important part of their television personality.

Now shuffle the shows and hosts around so that new pairs are created:

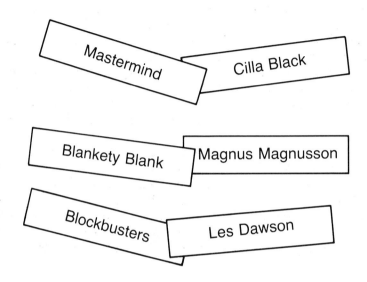

Would these new pairs work? Consider each one and discuss your reactions to them. What makes a successful combination and why do some not work? Think of real examples.

---

1 Take three game shows and imagine you have to write a job description for the host, explaining his or her role and detailing what has to be done.

2 Imagine that the present host of each show has to leave, and you must hire another famous name as a replacement. Write a letter to the interview panel saying who you would recommend for the job and why.

PUBLIC APPEAL

As we have already seen, game shows are hugely popular. Many of them originate in America, and they can be seen with different variations throughout much of the world. Others come from nearer to home, for example, 3-2-1 began life in Spain as *Tres-Dos-Uno*. Each country adapts a show to suit their national audience whilst keeping the basic theme which is its selling point. Not all these adaptations are successful; the relentless Japanese game show *Ultra Quiz* proved a dismal flop when it appeared in Britain a few years ago.

Here, **Gill Stribling-Wright** discusses some of the ideas behind the highly successful game show *Blind Date*:

We make all our own game shows in Britain: why don't we import them, like we do with cop shows and soap operas?
I think you can identify more easily with your own national types – everyone sees something familiar in the contestants. In *Blind Date*, you'll be thinking, 'If I was there, I'd choose number one . . .', or 'I bet she'll go for number three . . .', and you see how funny it is if the contestant chooses a particular type.

You feel part of a show made with your own people; you don't care about the American public in the same way you care about your own. The people in cop shows and soap operas are just actors – like pin-ups and rock stars – they're universal, they belong to everybody. But ordinary people don't, somehow. They're people you know, or someone just like them.

We also have our own sense of humour. If we looked at an American or an Australian game show, or if they looked at a British one, they wouldn't necessarily understand why certain things were funny. Every country has its own brand of humour. The British are very good at taking the mickey out of things. They wouldn't play unless they thought it was a bit of a joke. On the other hand, the Dutch and the Germans make their versions more serious. They say they'd never get contestants to be as honest as the British couples. They want something more serious, more polite, and they want to get a marriage out of it.

/ *Cilla Black on the set of* Blind Date

There are so many game shows, what has made Blind Date *such a big success?*
It's what everybody does: everybody goes on dates. Love, courtship, marriage – it happens all the time to everybody, young and old. And if it's not happening to you, you can see it happening to other people. You can go to a party and see some guy talking to some girl, and you weigh up the chances. People sit on the sidelines watching. You hear people discussing last night's date in offices, in pubs, all the time. In the same way, people tune in to *Blind Date* to see how a couple got on. They've built up an interest in the process; they feel involved in making the match. People seem to enjoy that callback business better than anything else.

What happens if you have to find a new host?
You'd have to find out who was available. It wouldn't automatically have to be someone of the same sex. You'd have to find someone else who could strike the right tone. If the game itself is strong enough, it will always survive a change of host. It's the process you're looking at, the host simply enhances it. People might say a show was better in the good old days before the change of host, but they still tune in. You have to give the new host a chance to do something a little different, to do things their own way. It's not fair to walk in the old host's footsteps; if you tried to do exactly the same thing, you wouldn't develop the strengths of the new personality.

Gill Stribling-Wright, producer of Blind Date

PRACTICAL ASSIGNMENT

In this exercise, you record a short quiz. You will need two contestants, a camera operator, a host and a host's assistant. The host will need seven questions (three each and one tie-breaker). Arrange a suitable set and put the camera where it has a clear view of contestants and host.

Rehearse the following moments in advance and decide how you are going to deal with them:

- How the contestants are introduced
- How the host explains the game and the rules
- How the host copes with a wrong answer
- What happens when a contestant wins
- How the host finishes the show

Afterwards . . .

Watch your performance on the screen and discuss the following points:

- What went on in your head at the time
- How you managed the rehearsed moments listed above
- What personal qualities and skills are possessed by the ideal host

VIEWING ASSIGNMENT

Watch a game show, and as you watch keep a viewing journal (see page 99), noting down your changing responses as the show progresses. In particular, notice where your sympathies lie, and when you 'join in'. Can you account for the way your viewpoint changes?

Now consider the experience from the point of view of one of the contestants. Stop the tape occasionally and suggest how the contestant's 'thought bubbles' would sound if we could listen in on them. Do the same for the host. Not all these 'thought bubbles' will be as cheery as the image we usually expect. Why not?

TRY IT YOURSELF

Think up a new game show and prepare a portfolio of material to send to television stations, as a way of selling the idea to them. Include:

- an outline of how the game works and what is new and interesting about it
- factual information such as the title, who would host it and when it would be shown
- a sample of the questions
- a sketch of the set, complete with scoreboards, props, etc.
- an entry for the *TV Times* or *Radio Times* introducing the first programme

Sport

INTRODUCTION

The televising of sport is full of problems for those who make programmes. Some of them arise because:

- events take place away from the studio
- they often happen out of doors
- they are not always predictable
- events only happen once

What are the other problems that arise?

Choose *three* different sporting events and make a list of all the problems which may occur, and how you might deal with them.
    For example, at an *athletics meeting*:

(a) **It might rain**
- crew get wet
  equipment gets wet
  meeting called off

Do you
- put on an old film instead?
  take a lot of waterproofing?
  show last year's meeting?

(b) **Several events clash**
Do you
- record them all and show some later?
  record only the most exciting?
  try to follow several events at once by cutting between them?

CAMERAWORK

The **camera crew** set up and operate the cameras.

An **outside broadcast** van full of equipment is driven to the event and the pictures from each camera are shown on screens inside the van.

The **director** chooses which pictures to show. This is a tough job if the event is being shown live, because decisions have to be made on the spur of the moment.

Here, sports director, **John Scriminger**, discusses some problems of televising sport:

Television has given sport a wider audience. Eight million people can see a Cup Final on television whilst only 90,000 of them can get into Wembley. A lot of sports that wouldn't normally be seen are promoted by television. Badminton and netball are two examples. Smaller sports have benefited.

Most sports can be televised. We do try to cover the whole range – I've done orienteering and cross-country archery, for example – but some lend themselves better than others. Pistol-shooting is a fine sport, but dull for the viewer just watching holes appear on a target. And squash is very difficult to televise – the ball is too small and the pace is too fast to see clearly on the small screen.

You can reach saturation point with some sports. At one time you could see show-jumping on television three or four times every week. It killed itself by over-exposure. Snooker is reaching that point.

Pictures which are sent to us from stations in other countries can tend to cover the home competitors to the exclusion of the rest. The Americans were guilty of this during the Los Angeles Olympics. We didn't see our own athletes coming in second because all the cameras were on the American who came in first. This is bad direction. The fact is that you can't actually get the viewer there. There's nothing like being there – the Olympics, the World Championships; you can't recreate that atmosphere on screen. Our responsibility is to represent the whole event fairly. Even when we have one of our favourite people participating, we must give fair coverage of the whole event. Viewers don't want to miss a thrilling battle for second place because the camera is dwelling on the winner. Of course, the director can only see what the cameras are showing. You rely on the camera operator finding an interesting picture and offering it to you.

Another limitation is that you are dealing with instant decisions made on the spot. Most outside broadcasts are live. You have to live with the shot you choose at the time, good or bad: you can't go back and have another look at it. The most hectic broadcast I ever did was a Brands Hatch Grand Prix which lasted three hours. With 12 cameras covering fast-moving cars, the experience was exhausting; it felt like three days.

You also have to live with technical problems. The worst event I ever had was when four of my five cameras broke down ten seconds before we went on air. We had to make do with one camera for the first five minutes. Another time we lost all pictures just as we went on air. In a case like that you just carry on as though nothing has happened and hope that the audience will bear with you until the pictures are restored.

John Scriminger, Senior Sports Director, LWT

TRY IT YOURSELF

One of the most important decisions is where to put the available cameras, so that viewers at home have a good view of events.

Imagine you are a director with a camera crew. This month you are to go with your crew to make live programmes for certain sporting events. In each case, you have a plan of the ground (pp. 35–8) and a list of the available equipment. Study the information carefully and then mark in where you would put the cameras, and at what height.

What things do you have to bear in mind in choosing the location of the cameras? Make a list.

```
┌─────────────────────────────────────────┐
│                  SEATS                    │
└─────────────────────────────────────────┘

┌──────┐  ┌─────────────────────────┐  ┌──────┐
│      │  │                         │  │      │
│      │  │                         │  │      │
│      │  │                         │  │      │
│      │  │                         │  │      │
│ Rest │  │                         │  │      │
│ area │  │                         │  │      │
│  □   │  │                         │  │      │
│ SEATS│  │■○━━━━━━━━━━━━━━━━━━━○     │  │SEATS │
│      │  │Umpire        NET        │  │      │
│  □   │  │                         │  │      │
│ Rest │  │                         │  │      │
│ area │  │                         │  │      │
│      │  │                         │  │      │
│      │  │                         │  │      │
│      │  │                         │  │      │
└──────┘  └─────────────────────────┘  └──────┘
```

TENNIS COURT

Equipment available:

4 cameras
1 scaffold

```
┌─────────────────────────────────────────┐
│                  SEATS                    │
└─────────────────────────────────────────┘

┌─────────────────────────────────────────┐
│               SCOREBOARD                  │
└─────────────────────────────────────────┘
```

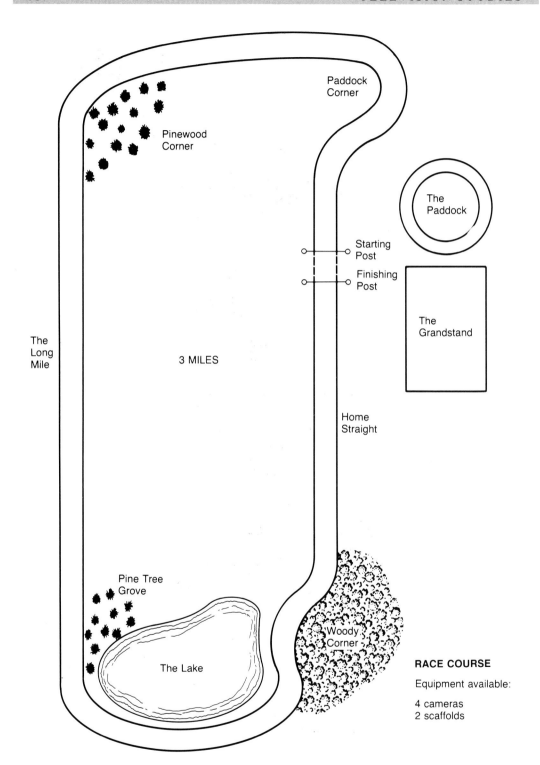

Paddock
Corner

Pinewood
Corner

The
Paddock

Starting
Post

Finishing
Post

The
Grandstand

The
Long
Mile

3 MILES

Home
Straight

Pine Tree
Grove

Woody
Corner

The Lake

RACE COURSE

Equipment available:

4 cameras
2 scaffolds

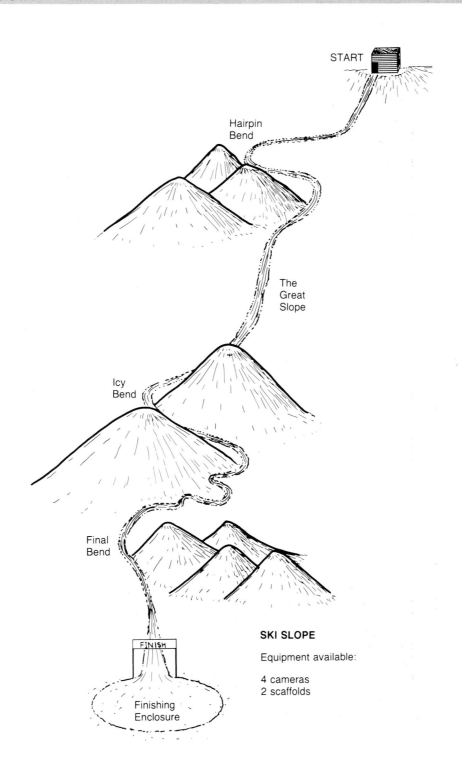

START

Hairpin
Bend

The
Great
Slope

Icy
Bend

Final
Bend

FINISH

Finishing
Enclosure

SKI SLOPE

Equipment available:

4 cameras
2 scaffolds

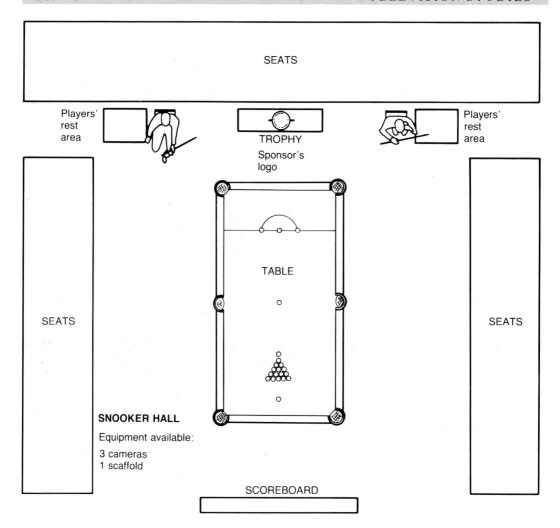

SEATS

Players' rest area

TROPHY
Sponsor's logo

Players' rest area

SEATS

TABLE

SEATS

SNOOKER HALL

Equipment available:

3 cameras
1 scaffold

SCOREBOARD

PRACTICAL ASSIGNMENT

Choose a short sporting event as the subject of your video – a long-jump competition, for example. When you are experienced, you can try this exercise with games which last over a longer period, cover more ground and involve more people. They require quite sophisticated camerawork.

- Go out and make a map of the area.
- Decide where to put the camera or cameras and show this on the map.
- Rehearse. Find out what will happen and when, then plan what pictures to take. Avoid waste. Decide at what points to start and stop the recordings. Get someone to rehearse the event for the camera operator, to check that there is a clear view.
- Record the event.

Afterwards . . .

Discuss what you have learnt from this experience, in particular:

- How do you choose what to show if you can't show the whole event?
- In what way is the video different from the actual event? Does it feel the same when you watch it on video?
- What are the limitations of televised sport?

Here, **John Scriminger** offers his advice on the coverage of some sports events:

At an *athletics meeting* you must show a clear view of the finish line and the various starting points for the track events, and reasonable coverage of the field events. Some cameras will have to do double duty by showing, say, the final bend of the 400 metres as well as the start of the long jump. You've also got to allow for the fact that some of the running and throwing events change direction depending on the wind speed.

At a *tennis match*, you have to have a clear view of the service and the court lines so that the viewer can judge whether the ball is in or out. You've also got to be able to show close-ups of the players, both during play and while they're sitting at the umpire's chair between sets. The best place is behind one or other of the servers.

In *badminton*, which is a similar kind of game but much faster, it's best to shoot diagonally across the court, to capture the running back and forth. With all net sports the camera height is important – you must be careful not to obscure any court lines with the top of the net. And don't have the cameras all at the same height or it looks very boring.

For a *football match*, it's ideal to have two cameras on the centre line, one for close-ups and the other for full game coverage. In addition, use a low-angle camera for other close-ups of players and certainly a camera behind each goal for reverse angle shots. They're the ones most often used for slow-motion replays. One very important point is that they must all be on the same side of the pitch, or when you cut between cameras the players will suddenly change direction!

 # VIEWING ASSIGNMENT

Watch 5–10 minutes of a sporting event. Try to work out where the cameras are. Make a map of the pitch or circuit, and mark on it the position of the cameras.

Afterwards . . .

Discuss what reasons the director may have had for putting the cameras where they were.

News and Current Affairs

INTRODUCTION

Although most people recognise that newspapers have their own political sympathies and choose those which fit in with their own outlook, there is a common belief that television news is somehow free from bias.

What we think of as news has been carefully selected beforehand. What counts as an important story is someone's decision. A certain type of news tends to be shown – news which is eye-catching, action-packed, and only just happened. A rowdy picket line makes for more dramatic pictures than the weeks of discussion which precede it – but is it better news? A famine in the Third World has been going on for years, and we've seen the pictures a hundred times before – but is it less important now? People love to see celebrities going about their business – but is that really news? News does not happen, it is chosen.

TRY IT YOURSELF

News is made quickly. Programmes are put together at the last minute from the reports which are sent in during the day. The news team has to make snap decisions about what to include and how to present it.

Imagine yourself in charge of the evening news. It is nearly time for the news bulletin, when last-minute problems arise. What you have to do is:

- discuss the problem with your news team and make a list of all the possible courses of action
- choose one
- be prepared to say why you chose it

1 Your big news story about a military invasion is all ready when you hear that the camera has failed: all you have is the sound of your on-the-spot reporter commenting on the pictures. You have **two minutes** to discuss the alternatives and make a decision.

2 A last-minute press release from Downing Street has accused one of your top reporters of political bias in the coverage of recent events in Northern Ireland. The morning newspapers will be buzzing with the news so it may be awkward to ignore it. How do you deal with it? You have **five minutes**.

3 You have received a hurried phone call from a very important person giving you first details of a major scandal about to break. It concerns a prominent member of the government. The story would be a scoop, but there is no time to check the information. What do you do? You have **two minutes**.

4 You are working on the last news item of the evening and there are two stories to choose from. One is a story of some political importance about a by-election, and the other is a funny story about a cat stranded up a tree. The trouble is, you have no pictures to go with the by-election story, but you do have them for the cat story. Which do you choose? You have **two minutes**.

5 Following an air disaster, your reporter has sent in pictures of distressed relatives arriving to identify the bodies. You know there is a lot of public interest in the disaster, and that other news services intend to show similar pictures. Is it right to show pictures of private grief? You have **three minutes**.

Afterwards . . .

List all the factors you took into account in making your decisions, and put them in order of importance.

MAKING NEWS

Some days there are so many events that the news services have to leave out a lot of stories which would otherwise be shown. When there is a lull in the news, it has to be found or built up from a small amount of information. On the day of a general election, for example, there is an awkward period when little happens, after the polls have closed but before the first results are in. The audience is eager for news of the election, but there is little to give.

Imagine yourselves as the team working on the election news service. You have a short gap to fill in that awkward period just after the polls have closed. Luckily you have some pictures which were recorded during the day, but at the moment they are too long and have no commentary. The pictures on pp. 42–3 each represent a few moments from the recording. You are in a rush and have to make a news story out of them to fill the gap.

Choose **eight** of the pictures on the next two pages for your news story and write a commentary to go with them.

Afterwards . . .

Compare the results of each group, noticing the range of stories possible. In particular, pay attention to the commentaries, which tell the viewer how to read the picture. Choose one picture in particular to see how many different interpretations have been

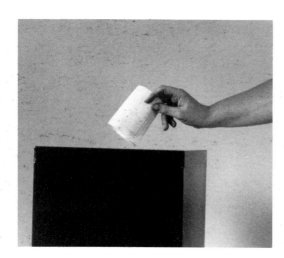

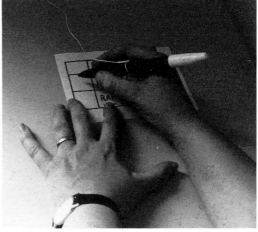

made of it. This exercise is important because people assume that pictures 'speak for themselves' – that the camera cannot lie.

To illustrate this point, turn the volume right down during part of a news bulletin and write the commentary which you imagine goes with the pictures. Listen to the same story with the volume turned up and compare your commentary with that of the newscaster.

PRACTICAL ASSIGNMENT

Suppose there are three news services, each one with its own aims, like this:

THE SUNSHINE SERVICE
Aims: to seek out good news, happy news, news
            of success
        to report the main events of the day
        to entertain as well as inform
        to keep it snappy

THE BULLDOG SERVICE
Aims: to provide expert analysis and comment
        to oppose violence and unpleasantness of
            all kinds
        to promote a proper respect for authority
        to inspire patriotism

THE BEACON SERVICE
Aims: to reveal the news behind the headlines
        no-nonsense reporting on issues of
            political importance
        to present a balanced view
        to be honest, accurate and fair

Get into three groups to represent each service. Bearing in mind your aims, choose from the material below which stories you are going to run in a five minute news broadcast. Put them into a running order that reflects their importance, deciding how long to spend on each one. You can use as much of the footage (video pictures) as you wish, cutting some out or adding in commentary as you like.

Material Available

PRIZE MARROW CONTEST
Amusing pictures of winning entries
Interview with winner – how I grew the Whopper

EVE OF BY-ELECTION
By-election tomorrow in 'safe' seat
Footage: candidates campaigning
Results of latest poll

CRICKET RESULTS
Three hours of footage: the big match
Interview with winning captain

MIDWIVES 'ONE-HOUR' STRIKE –
COUNTRYWIDE WALKOUT
No footage
Voice-only interview with patient affected

FOOTBALLING INJURY
Big name has sprained ankle – out of action
Footage: footballer being treated

FOOTBALL BIG MATCH
No score draw
Two hours of footage   – the match
                         – interviews
                         – half-time band

FAIRGROUND ACCIDENT
Child sprained ankle when ride started
    accidentally
Footage – several fairgrounds
        – the ride itself in action

NEAR-MISS AEROPLANE
SHOCK
Two aeroplanes nearly collide – faulty
    instruments
No pictures

MILITARY TAKE-OVER
On ex-Commonwealth island
Excellent five minute voice-only report

PENSIONS UP
Unexpected rise in Senior Citizens allowance
Fifteen minute interview with Prime Minister

NEW HOME FOR CATS OPENED
Footage – adorable pictures of saved pussies
        – lean strays on city streets

POP STAR SPOTTED ON
NUDE BATHING BEACH
Full frontal pictures

RECORD TEMPERATURES IN AUSTRALIA
Map available
Footage – bathing beach

DEBATE ON WORLD POVERTY
United Nations discussion
One hour footage – but in foreign languages –
    subtitles available

RESTAURANT FINED
Cat's paw found in soup
Pictures of manager leaving court – 'No
    comment'

SCHOOL CHEF OF THE YEAR
AWARD
Interview with winner
Pictures of winning menu
Comments by judges

DUTCH ELM DISEASE
Report on ongoing work to prevent spread of
    disease
Thirty seconds of footage – new treatments in
    tree injections

RADIATION AT SEA
Environmental group research into radiation
    levels near nuclear reactors
Footage of nuclear reactor

REPORT FROM SOUTH AMERICA
General report on state of major industries in
    South America
Footage of tin mines, etc.

400 JOBS LOST

Large international company closing down
    factory
Moving to another country
Footage – interview with managing director
        – pictures of workers reading
                redundancy notices
But interview with trade union representative
    fails to arrive in time for broadcast

EXPLOSION IN HOLIDAY HOTEL
Gas leak explosion in European seaside resort
Footage – dramatic pictures taken by passing
    tourist – but very poor quality

Prepare a list of items in the desired order indicating how long you will spend on each one. Underneath each item in your list, show a breakdown of what you would include in it:

e.g.   *Chosen story*

newscaster – outline of story	15 seconds
footage – the event	
– reporter on the spot giving details	45 seconds
	1 min total

Prepare to perform the broadcast on video or live to the rest of the class. Your broadcast must run for exactly five minutes to the second, so accurate timekeeping is essential. Time each story so that you will know as you go along whether you are on schedule. You will need:

– two or three newscasters
– reporters for 'on the spot' reports
– interviewees
– a timekeeper to keep reports on schedule
– a director to organise everyone
– a camera operator
– people to prepare the set

Some people will have to double up on jobs. Newscasters should prepare their scripts, interviewers write their own questions. It is the job of the director to organise other people to help out.

You may make up details about each story as you wish. You cannot provide action pictures, so simply refer to them and move on, deducting the time you would use on them from your allowance.

Save some of your time for rehearsals.

During recording, break between each contribution to allow the newscasters to gather their wits and the camera operator to shift the camera.

Afterwards . . .

Compare the three news broadcasts. Notice the different order and length of the stories, and the way they are presented.

Is it possible to make a news broadcast which is free from bias? Is there in fact a 'correct' view? This is a very important question, since people trust the news and judge the affairs of the world on the information it provides. The news affects the way all of us see the world.

News services realise there is a problem, and do their best to provide a 'balance' of views, though it isn't really possible to represent every opinion or to explain cases in the fullest detail. This means that minority views are under-represented, and an overall impression emerges that it is right to sit in the middle, rather than have strong opinions.

Current affairs programmes help to fill this gap by examining some issues in greater detail, especially by interviewing the people involved so that they can speak for themselves. One of the difficulties of the ordinary news bulletin is capturing someone's arguments in a few sentences. Politicians in particular play to the cameras by thinking up clever and pithy comments which they know will be easy to quote on the news. It comes over well on the screen – but does it do justice to the complex issues of running the country?

VIEWING ASSIGNMENT

Choose one news story on one particular evening and watch the way it is covered on three different channels. Make a note of:

- the length of the item
- where in the programme it appears (first? second? third?)
- the information given
- the pictures and interviews provided
- the tone or gist of the reporting

Write a brief report of your findings, and say which service in your opinion provided the best coverage and why.

Live Shows

INTRODUCTION

The first programmes made in television studios were all broadcast live. It was many years before the videotape recorder was invented and editing became possible. To modern eyes the programmes of those days seem unpolished, not just because of the blurry black-and-white pictures, but also because they were unedited; all the slips and technical hitches were transmitted as they happened.

Today we see polished performances which are pre-recorded so that problems can be removed in the editing. However, some programmes are still shown live. Chat shows and interviews are often transmitted live precisely because we don't want glossy, prepared images. We like to see politicians, for example, put on the spot. Perhaps we expect to hear a more honest answer this way, or maybe we are excited by the possibility of blunders. Live music and public events are also popular because we want to capture the feeling of being there, experiencing the events first hand.

Unfortunately, live television can disappoint the viewer who has come to expect the flawless performances of edited programmes. In these, every irrelevant moment is cut out so that we are left with an intense, action-packed drama compressed into the available time. When we watch a live programme, we have to put up with all the repetitions, mistakes and dull moments.

In an odd way, television has made everyday life seem grey. Characters in soap operas seem to live more intensely than we do; football highlights seem more dramatic and action-packed than real-life matches; comedians never dry up, jokes never fall flat, actors never forget their lines in edited television. Life isn't quite like that!

Live television shows, therefore, have a tough job because they have to live up to the standards set by edited programmes. They also need the exciting feeling of immediacy – of things happening here, now. It is this sense of involvement that is so hard to achieve and which must be carefully planned. If every mistake gets transmitted, things have to be organised to make mistakes unlikely.

TRY IT YOURSELF

Imagine you are responsible for a live show based on current music but also containing other material such as occasional interviews, comic sketches, dance routines, audience discussions, stand-up comedians and pop videos, and to which members of the public are admitted.

What will you need to bear in mind in planning the show? Though it may seem a simple matter to put the acts in order and point the cameras at them when the time comes, serious difficulties may arise on the night which must be anticipated in the planning. For example, moving musical equipment makes noise and takes time. What effect might this have on the order of acts? Cameras need a clear view of the performers. What limitations might this place on their location?

Anticipating the possible problems, design a set for the series described in the first paragraph of this section. Then prepare a plan for this week's programme giving:

– a running order
– camera locations (use three, mobile or fixed, as you wish)
– where on the set each act will appear
– how the acts will be linked or announced
– where the audience will stand/sit/dance

This week's acts will be:

– two sketches by comic trio
– pop video
– comic juggling act which involves members of the audience
– solo singer – two songs and interview, open to question and comment from the audience
– dance routine
– group playing hit single

The programme will last one hour.

Afterwards . . .

Consider the factors you took into account in designing the set and organising the show. Make a list and then put the factors in order of importance.

On page 50 there is a photograph showing the set of *Saturday Live*, a popular programme which was broadcast on Channel 4 at 10 pm on Saturdays.

The programme contained music which ranged from choirs to solo singers, as well as regular comic sketches and guest comedians. A large portion of the audience were seated, but many also danced or stood to watch the comic turns. Some of the cameras moved around the floor by clearing a path through the audience first. **Mike Oxley** explains how he designed it:

How did you go about designing the set?
I knew there would be two or three live bands each week, as well as stand-up comics and comedy sketches, so that was my starting point. I needed two definite band areas, a centre stage area for the stand-up comics, and an acting area. And room for the audience of course. So I sat up late one night thinking, and drawing some sketches, then I started building a model – a lot of people can't follow drawings so a model helps everyone to see what it will look like.

What was your first idea for the set?
I'd heard about this trend for holding parties in old warehouses, and I wanted to create
that kind of atmosphere – to make it look like a warehouse party but with an added fantasy
element – a stylised version of a really big exciting party. Originally I was going to make it
a Victorian warehouse, all old brick, but then I saw some photos of the old Firestone
factory which had just been demolished in West London, and I liked the 1930s' windows
so much I used that for inspiration. Then I started filling it with weird things – cars
coming out of the walls, giant inflatable hamburgers, neon lights. There was something
to look at all the way round the studio – not a bare bit of wall anywhere – and the
atmosphere was very good. People really loved it.

/ *The set of* Saturday Live

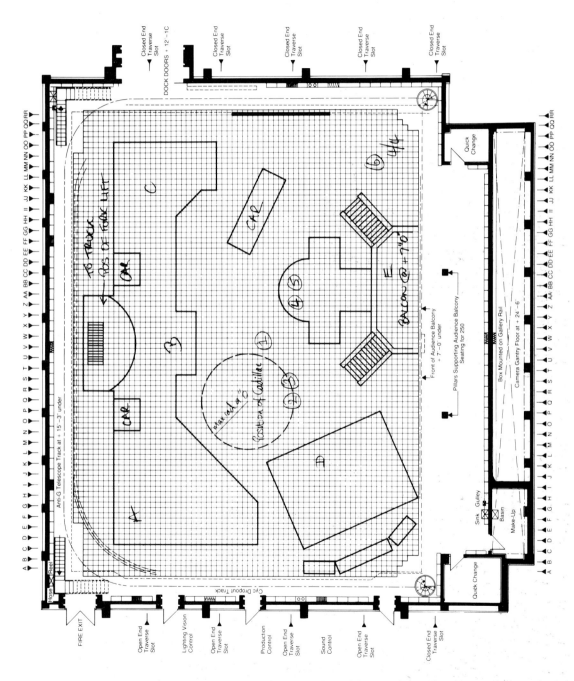

/ Floor plan of the Saturday Live set

What particular problems did you face with a live show?
Safety first of all. The audience were all over the set, and the cameras were constantly moving about. We used some professional 'shovers' – I think they're used by *Top of the Pops* – people who look as though they're part of the audience and who dance a bit, and they just try to shove people out of the way to clear a path for the camera. It's quite difficult really.

Wasn't it difficult to change sets during the show?
Not really. We moved small sets during the commercial breaks and while the bands were playing because there was plenty of noise then. Basically you need two or three different areas so that one can be set up while another one is 'on air'.

Did the set work as you hoped?
Yes, we were all really pleased that everything worked OK – with a live show so many things could go wrong, but nothing did. At the beginning the set was perhaps a bit bare, so we just added things as we went along. The audience tended to mass together in one big lump, which didn't look quite right, so we split them up by extending the island area in the middle. That worked well, although some of the comics were afraid of people standing behind them pulling faces. At the end of the last show, the set 'blew up' – with foam rubber bricks and rocks flying everywhere – I thought that would make a nice ending for the series!

Mike Oxley, set designer, Saturday Live

Swap set designs with someone else, and after a minute or so, interview each other about the design, and how it was achieved.

VIEWING ASSIGNMENT

Watch a live music programme for young people.
   As you watch, keep a note of the features which give the programme its lively, urgent atmosphere. Pay particular attention to:

   – the background (set, lighting, equipment in view)
   – the camerawork (especially the frequency of the cuts and the angle of the camera)
   – visual effects
   – the style of the presenters
   – the behaviour of the studio audience
   – the behaviour of performers

Afterwards, share your observations in groups.
   It is interesting to note the effect the things listed above have on the eye. Everything is in motion – especially the camera. Flashing lights, bizarre sets and video effects add to the impression of energy and excitement. Watch the way music is presented for the older generation and you don't find the same frantic pace. Young people are expected to enjoy the sensation of being 'blitzed' by the scene. It is hard to imagine a music programme which takes its time; everything seems to be happening here and now, and

is gone before there's time to consider. Although it is live, it has been carefully prepared to have that urgent feel. The crazy camera work, the sensational sets, the restless pace and the flashing lights are all manufactured. Pop programmes are one of the most vivid forms of television – and one of the few where we see the cameras, microphones and set construction – but like the rest of television, someone planned it that way.

PRACTICAL ASSIGNMENT

For the practical assignment, we turn to another common form of live programme, the interview or chat show. You will have to find a topic for discussion which is important to all of you, perhaps something in the news which is of general interest, or a local issue, even a school or college matter. The video will consist of an interview with one person, to be followed by questions and contributions from a panel of eight people. You will need:

- a camera operator
- an interviewer
- a guest to be interviewed
- a panel of eight people with differing opinions to contribute ideas and questions after the interview

Prepare the set against a blank wall:

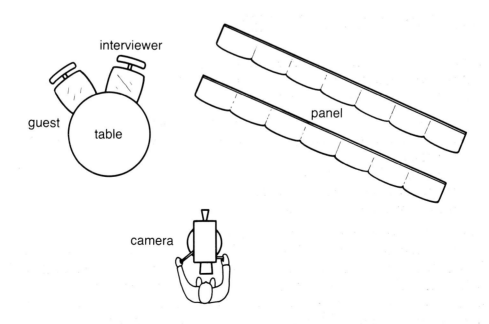

Divide into three groups – one to prepare the set and the camera, one to prepare questions, and another for the panel to have a warm-up discussion to get ideas flowing. Next, rehearse the order of events step by step before making the video. This will help the camera operator and the interviewer who need to know where and when to move. Finally, record the video without pauses.

Before viewing the video, write down your private feelings about the experience.

After viewing the video, write down your reactions to seeing your own performance on the screen.

In groups, discuss your reactions to the video as a whole:

– Consider how the guest interview might appear if it were edited. If you had to cut it down to half its length, how would you decide what to cut out?
– Go further now, and decide what you would select if you only had the time to show two or three sentences, as they do in the news.
– Try to arrive at some conclusions about the problems of live performance, firstly for the participants, secondly for the interviewer, thirdly for the technical crew and finally for the viewer.

For homework . . .

Watch out for interviews on television in the coming week. Chat shows always feature interviews, but you can often find them in the news and current affairs programmes. Make a note of the programme title and decide whether the interview has been edited or not. The important point here is how you arrived at your decision. What are the clues which tell you if an interview has been edited? You may be surprised how little live television you see.

At the end of the week, discuss the interviews you have seen:

– Which were live? How do you know?
– Do you think some speakers come over better in television interviews than others? What is their secret?
– What are the qualities of a good interviewer?
– Is there any way of knowing that the speakers have been fairly represented?

PART TWO / *Making Meaning*

Most of us don't stop to consider where television comes from – we just turn on the set and there it is. On first impressions, television seems to offer a window on the world. We can see events as they happen, and this leads us to think we are seeing the unvarnished truth, something we particularly want with regard to news coverage. We expect television to be impartial, indeed the Broadcasting Acts require it to be so. But no television in the world is actually unbiased in this way.

Every image we see has been selected, every camera angle has been chosen, every sound considered. Someone has put the shots in order, added a voice-over, cut out certain pictures, added in certain sounds. To some extent, all television is biased because it is has been manufactured in some or all of these ways. This is no deliberate fraud; it is an inevitable part of the process.

The people who make television programmes are limited in what they can do, not just by practical problems such as cash and time, but also by tradition. Television audiences expect programmes to make sense in the usual way, as do the people making them. It is easier to get things done if everyone keeps to familiar ground rules, but it does mean that real changes are slow to happen.

In this section, we look at some of the ways in which programmes are put together, and how this affects the meaning of them. It is important to understand that there is a language in the pictures and sounds of television, ways of ordering and linking them which we barely notice because we are so used to them. And it may come as a surprise that a few moments of slick television can take weeks of planning and compromise. What gets on to television is limited by very practical considerations such as cost, time and availability. Even when we sit down to watch the programme, we do not see it in complete innocence: more often than not our expectations have been primed by previews, promotions and even by title sequences.

This section, then, aims to reveal some of the ways in which television makes its meanings.

Reading Television

READING PICTURES

Look at the pictures below for a few moments. Make a private note of:

- what you imagine happened just before
- what is happening now
- what you expect to happen next
- what you can tell about the people
- what you can tell about the places
- where you, the observer, seem to watch from

Compare answers.

Explain which details or clues led to your conclusions. How do you account for different interpretations?

Now look at the cartoon on pages 57–8. Here, each picture has a 'before' and 'after', so one can be more confident about interpretations. Work out your answers to the following questions:

- How much time passes between each picture?
- What do you imagine happening between each picture?
- Where do you, the eye watching the scene, seem to be?

Notice how your imagination fills in the gaps between the pictures, and adjusts to changes in time, place and viewpoint. It uses all the information it receives to make sense of the story.

TELEVISION GRAMMAR

Watching television seems effortless, but the brain is busy all the time piecing together information and making meaning from it.

Watch a few minutes of television.

Notice that the camera is not left running in one long shot and that what you hear is not always the natural background sound to the picture. Then answer the questions below:

1 There are several ways of breaking off from one shot and moving to the next. Can you put a name to them? Find an example of each and say if you can see a difference in what they mean.
2 Often the break between pictures means that time has passed. Find an example, saying what happens in the meantime and how you know. Why do you suppose it was left out?
3 Find an example of a picture break in which no time has passed. Why then is there a break?

We learn to 'read' television in the same way we learn any kind of language, picking up the rules as we go along. Once we are familiar with them, we barely notice they are there. But in our heads we are busy forging information from the screen into an understanding of the programme.

PRACTICAL ASSIGNMENT

The following are short exercises for groups using a video camera. The quality of the acting is not very important since the main point here is to notice how shots are put together. Do the exercises one at a time: in this way you will learn from your mistakes as you go along. Discuss each exercise first, planning your shots and saving time for discussion afterwards. Although these exercises look simple, be warned that it will probably take quite a while to solve the problems they pose. Putting your finger on exactly what is wrong is more difficult than you imagine.

1   Choose someone in the group who is unable to play the piano, and create a ten second video in which he or she appears to play a masterpiece.
    There are several ways of doing this. Which is most convincing?

2   Record a conversation between two people who appear to be face to face in the same room, but who are in fact located in two separate rooms.
    It is easy to create such illusions on television. In the same way, for example, we can have the illusion that a conversation staged in London happened in Glasgow. It can save a lot of time and money.

3   Choose someone to be a magician. Provide a box or a top hat, from which the magician pulls an amazing number of objects.
    How are you going to do this? Simple: cheat. Stop and start the camera to pop new items into the hat. This should be simple enough. The problem is that the viewer can usually spot these moments because of small movements and changes in the picture. Can you think of ways round this?

4   Get one person to walk from the classroom to another spot in the building such as the library. Time the walk. Now record the same walk onto video in one quarter of the time it takes. So, if it takes one minute to get to the library, your video must last only 15 seconds.
    You will realise that television programmes do this all the time. To include every moment would be boring and irrelevant. So how do you bluff the viewer about ground not covered, yet give a clear impression of the full walk?

Afterwards . . .

Discuss the results and compare the merits of different versions. Pinpoint the moments which do not seem to work, and consider how else you might have done them. If you cannot work out quite what is wrong, watch out for similar moments on broadcast television. These exercises will cast a new light on your television viewing. You will be astonished how often these simple tricks are used. We don't notice them in day-to-day viewing because we are so used to them. They are television *conventions* – ways of doing things which everyone accepts.

VIEWING ASSIGNMENT

It is interesting to note that these conventions – the accepted rules of television presentation – vary from country to country, and change subtly over a period of time.

1 Watch a conversation between two people in an American soap opera, and compare it with a similar conversation in an English soap opera. What differences do you notice in the camerawork?

2 Compare the way new scenes are opened in a British soap opera and an American soap opera.

3 New technology has made possible new visual effects. Pictures can be flipped, tumbled or shattered, for example. Watch out for these visual effects over the next few evenings and make a note when they appear and what impact they have. Do they 'mean' anything, in the same way that a picture cut might mean that time has passed?

4 Pictures are only one part of television: sound is the other, and it too obeys certain conventions. It can also be edited and added to, as it is for example with commentaries, sound effects and music. Watch a variety of programmes with the volume turned right down. For example:

– an item on the news
– a scene from a comedy
– a title sequence
– an advertisement

What words and music do you expect to hear when you listen to them with the volume up? Compare your answers with the actual soundtrack. How close was your guess? Of course you weren't guessing; you knew from experience what to expect. The pictures were full of clues – gestures, expressions, setting and so on. What clues did you use in the extracts you watched? Prepare a brief report of your findings.

Stock Events

INTRODUCTION

Stock events are the typical scenes you expect to see when you watch a certain type of programme. If you watch a Western you expect a shoot-out; if you watch a cop thriller you expect a car chase; if you watch a vampire story you eventually expect to see a bat hovering behind the billowing net curtains of the French windows which will shortly blow open in the inevitable thunderstorm.

You have detailed expectations of these familiar scenes. Take this one from a Western:

Our hero rides into town. The street is dusty and deserted. All he hears (always a *he!*) is the sound of voices and music from the saloon. *Which musical instrument does he hear?* He approaches the saloon, leaves his horse and enters the saloon. *How does he secure his horse?* As he enters, the company falls silent, the music grinds to a halt, and they all stare at the stranger in the doorway. *What sort of door is it?* Our hero brazens out the silence and approaches the bar. Gradually talk is resumed and the music strikes up. Our hero orders a drink. *What does he order?* Close to the bar, a number of evil-looking men are playing a game. *What game? What shape of table? What covering is on the table? What lighting?* The atmosphere is not good. An argument blows up. *What has triggered the bad feeling?* A fight develops. At first just two men are brawling, but within seconds everyone is involved, including our hero. Several pieces of furniture are broken, usually because they have been used as weapons, smashed over someone's head. *Which type of furniture is the most popular weapon of this sort?* People are beaten up and hurled around, and some of them end up outside. *How do they make their exit?* The brawling spreads upstairs. There are men fighting on the balcony. Most of them return to the ground floor the hard way. *How do they descend?* The dancing girls spill out onto the balcony. *How are they dressed?* Tempers reach a peak, and bullets start flying. The bartender has gone through all the emotions by this stage – anger, anxiety and now fear. *How does he protect himself?* The bar area itself is hardly a good place to hide. *What happens to the bottle shelves? What is behind the bottle shelves? How do they meet their end?* Finally, the entire company lies sprawled across the bar floor except for the most villainous man of all, who lies quivering at the feet of our hero, who has single-handedly put an end to the fight, put the local ring of baddies in their place and restored law and order. They watch in awed silence as he leaves without a word. His horse has not budged. Our hero rides off. *Into what?*

You may like to discuss the stock events of other genres. What stock events do you know from:

– horror?	– cop shows?
– science fiction?	– James Bond films?

CAMERA SEQUENCES

It is not only the events we predict in stock scenes, but also the way they are shown on the screen. A car chase would not be a car chase without a close-up of a squealing tyre, a cloud of dust as the car skids round in a U-turn, and a close-up of the dustbins it scatters on its way.

On pages 64–5 there are some camera shots from *Dempsey and Makepeace*, a popular detective series made by London Weekend Television.

Each shot represents a few seconds of moving video pictures.

1 Mentally arrange the shots into an order which will make sense as part of a story.

2 Record the order of shots in the margin of your photocopy.

3 Next to each shot write a brief explanation of what is going on to make clear the storyline.

4 Before looking at other people's work, consider the following questions:

- Would it be possible to tell your story in fewer shots, i.e. could you edit out some pictures and still tell the same story? Try it.
- Could you change the order of the shots to tell a different story? Try it.

5 Now compare your story with those of other people. Notice what all the versions have in common, and what varies.

- Can you account for the similarities?
- What factors limit the ordering of the shots?
- Would the same limits apply to the programme maker?

PRACTICAL ASSIGNMENT

Get into groups of three or four and discuss how you could set up a similar 'chase' scene indoors, with a view to making a two-minute video. You will need:

- a pursuer
- the pursued
- someone to operate the camera

Other members of the group may be the director or have extra parts in the video.

There is no need to explain the reason for the chase, or who the people are. Start your video in mid-chase.

- Plan a route.
- Check it with your teacher.
- Don't rush off yet . . .

Have a two-minute silence. In your mind run through a picture of the chase as it might appear on the video screen, noticing where your 'camera-eye' watches from, and picking out any special events or details which spring to mind. These observations will help to decide where to put the real camera, and what to include in each shot.

Take it in turn to describe to the others what you have seen in your mind's eye, drawing particular attention to the pace, angle and detail of the images. Pick out the best ideas and make a list of shots. The purpose of this list is to keep an overall plan in mind.

Now go off with your list and the camera to record the scene. Rehearse each shot first. Watch each 'take' on the instant playback and re-record shots which do not work before moving on.

When you have finished, invite people outside your group to join you in viewing and commenting on the video. After watching everyone's efforts, you may notice that the indoor chase has its own stock features. List them.

VIEWING ASSIGNMENT

Watch a popular *cartoon*. List or draw the stock events.

Who Does What and When

INTRODUCTION

Unlike novels and poems, a television programme is created by a group of people working as a team. We may know the name of a favourite actor, or sometimes the writer or even the director, but not many people look out for those who do the lighting, design the set, edit the videotape or work the camera. At the end of each programme you may see a list of people involved in the making of it. Think for a moment. Can you remember what jobs appear in the credits? Make a list and discuss what these jobs are.

PREPARATIONS

Before a programme gets as far as the studio, a lot of work has already been done. Many people have been busy thinking up ideas, hiring staff, organising money and resources as well as designing the set and the costumes. In this account, producer **Gill Stribling-Wright** describes the origins of the game show *Blind Date*:

> Like most game shows, the idea originated in America. A lot of countries do spin-off versions of it, but not always in the best taste! There were already versions in Australia and America, and most of Europe has followed suit since the success of *Blind Date*. Looking around for ideas for new shows is part of the Controller of Light Entertainment's job: the first I heard of *Blind Date* was when he called me into his office and showed me snippets of two foreign game shows about dating, and suggested we make a pilot version along the same lines.
>
> What always happens then is that we go away and think about it, and have a certain amount of discussion. The most important thing is the host – that's the one ingredient which is continuous. Who is the right person to host it? My first reaction, for some reason, was that it should be a woman. Abroad they use men, but Cilla was absolutely perfect for the show, she strikes just the right pitch. So choosing the host came straight away.
>
> Something else we discussed was the tone of the programme. We wanted people to see the funny side – dating is a very funny business, isn't it? – so we needed a host who would reflect this; not just a 'policeman' to move and marshall people around but someone who would be a lot of fun.
>
> At the same time, we had to make some adjustments to the format. The idea of one person questioning three others at the other side of the screen was fixed from the start, but recalling the guests to see how they got on was something we did because it was a weekly

show. Some overseas versions run five nights a week and they just occasionally have a couple coming back. They say 'Do you remember so and so from a few weeks ago . . . ?', and they have to remind you who they are. But the British like to see fair play, they want to know what happened to the other couples, so we decided to call them all back after their date.

The programme slot was obvious from the start: it was a show for peak-time viewing. I work in Light Entertainment, and that's what light entertainment is for. We are the 'front line troops' – we go in there and hook the viewers, to win their attention for the evening. So I immediately thought of it as early evening prime time viewing.

The next thing was to find a production team – a director, assistants, stage manager and so on. Particularly important were the people who designed the set, the lighting and the sound. In *Blind Date* everything depends upon hearing the contestants clearly, and seeing them all, even though they mustn't see each other until the final moment when the screen moves back.

Of course, we had to find people to take part. Researchers look for them. They think of the sort of people we're looking for and they ring up sports clubs, restaurant-discos, that sort of thing, and ask if they've got people interested. The manager will often ask around, and then the researcher will go along and select some contestants. Once a show is on air, we don't have to seek them out – people queue up to get on it.

The pilot show is seen by the head of the department and the director of programmes and a decision is made whether to run it or not. They decided *Blind Date* was worth making. The IBA approved it, too. So we went ahead and made the first series. It was a great success and as you know, several more series have been made since.

Gill Stribling-Wright, producer of *Blind Date*

PRODUCTION

Once the idea for the programme has taken shape, attention turns to the actual recording. This may be in a studio or an outside broadcast.

Look for a moment at the sketch on page 68 of a busy studio, and then consider the job titles given below. Can you match the people with the jobs?

Producer – overall organiser

Director – responsible for details of acting, camerawork and editing

Production Assistant – assists director, especially with timing

Vision mixer – switches between cameras under supervision of director

Actors

Lighting crew

Sound crew

Wardrobe supervisor

Make-up artist

Floor manager – responsible for organising people and passing on the director's instructions to the studio floor

Camera crew

Scenery crew

Stage manager – responsible for props and set

You can check your answers on p. 71.

/ The studio floor

POST PRODUCTION

Although some programmes are made on film, most are made and transmitted on videotape. The following extract explains what happens to the recorded material before it reaches the screen. Some words have been deleted from the account. Some of these are single words, and some are whole phrases. In a group, discuss which words would best fit in the gaps:

After work is finished in the studio or on the outside broadcast, there is still a lot to be done. Most of this will involve the help of a videotape (1). Together with the director, this person will cut out unwanted material and arrange the remainder in the best order.

Some of the material is of no use because the actors make mistakes and the director calls for a (2), and the recording begins again. The wasted bits – known as (3) – are sometimes used to entertain audiences on programmes such as (4).

There are other reasons why material is cut out. Some of it may appear more boring or (5) than was hoped. The (6) may not be up to scratch; for example, the lighting may be inadequate, the sound poor, or the picture may include unwanted details such as (7). A good editor can help to get round these problems by finding alternative pictures and sounds to create a similar effect. Sometimes material is not used because better shots are available on another tape. It is not unusual to have the programme recorded onto a master tape, but also to have a second tape, called the (8) tape which shows the same material but from a different angle, taken with another camera.

Another more urgent reason for editing the material is to fit it into the time allowed. Most programmes are less than (9) long. Every second is carefully timed, especially on ITV channels where some programmes go out to other parts of the country. The other channels in the (10) will want to know exactly when the programmes stop and start, so that they can insert their (11).

The recorded material will not always be in the best order. Programme makers find it more convenient to shoot scripts out of order so that they don't have to keep (12) particular studios, actors and outside locations. It means less trouble and less (13) if they get all the pictures they need from one place on one day. Instead, the scenes are shuffled into the right order at a later date by the editor. At this stage, there may well be other material to include, such as photographs and film extracts. These have to be transferred onto (14) before they can be transmitted on television.

Sounds may be added or changed – this process is called (15). Some programmes add a commentary – this is known as a (16). Music or other sound effects may be added. Visual effects such as (17) and fading may be used between scenes. Digital effects may be used to squash, twist, shatter or (18) the picture.

A (19) will be added to the beginning of the programme and (20) to the end.

All this is called post-production, because it happens after the actual recording. More and more time is being spent on it, as machines become more capable and the effects more polished.

You may like to check your chosen words with a teacher, or compare them with those selected by other groups, before checking them against the list of professional terms provided on p. 71.

When the programme is complete, it waits on tape until it is time to be transmitted, sometimes many months. In this time, advance publicity will attempt to arouse public interest in the programme. There will be previews and promotions and articles about it.

The transmission itself is supervised by the Transmission Controller in the Presentation Control Room. He or she keeps split-second timing of the schedule and directs the continuity announcer who bridges the gaps between programmes. A host of technical staff are also involved – engineers who run the film or videotape machines and Master Control engineers who overlook the technical quality of the transmission.

Considering the number of people involved, disasters are rare, though sometimes a machine breaks or the timing falters. In these emergencies it is the job of the Transmission Controller to put up a caption apologising for the delay.

After the programme is over, it may be reviewed in newspapers or on television

/ The Master Control Room

itself. If a programme is particularly successful, it becomes big business; books, tee-shirts, mugs and portraits can make a lot of money. The most successful programmes get repeated or a new series is made.

ANSWERS

Production

1 wardrobe supervisor
2 vision mixer
3 stage manager
4 producer
5 lighting crew
6 make-up artist
7 director
8 actors
9 camera crew
10 floor manager
11 sound crew
12 scenery crew
13 production assistant

Post production

The following technical terms are used by television staff, though you may have got the right idea using your own words. There are a range of possible answers to the other questions, so pool ideas in class.

1 editor
2 retake
3 outtakes
8 slave
10 network
14 videotape
15 dubbing
16 voice-over
19 title sequence
20 credits

TRY IT YOURSELF

Imagine you are a producer preparing for the following programmes:

- a few episodes of a soap opera already running and popular
- one programme in a travel series which features a different country each week

The programmes have to be ready for transmission in ten weeks. Draw up your plans. Firstly, use the illustrations below to make a list of staff whose services you will require. Put an asterisk (*) next to the staff who will be particularly important to you. Secondly, draw up a weekly calendar and write in a schedule of jobs to be completed.

Into the Can

INTRODUCTION

The French have a word for it – réalisation. It means to make something real, to bring it from an idea to an actual event. It is the job of the producer to have an idea for a television programme and bring it to life on the screen. The problems can be endless: money, equipment, places and people limit what can be done, and the producer has to make many compromises.

TELEVISATION

It is not always easy to get an idea onto the screen. For example, what problems would you anticipate in televising the following plays and how might you resolve them?

- a play set during a heatwave
- a play set in another century
- a play which follows the life of the central character from cradle to grave
- a play about the life and loves of a famous living person
- a play about an earthquake

Television has ways of dealing with these problems, with differing degrees of success. For instance, some events are made to happen off the screen or get cut out altogether. Perhaps the events are not shown in a traditional 'realistic' style, and the imagination has to stretch a little further.

TRY IT YOURSELF

Read the extract opposite and decide how you would go about bringing it to the screen.

March 20. A cold spring morning. It rained last night, perforating the crusted snow of the Tates' front lawn, and everything is wet and glitters: the fine gravel of the drive, the ice in the ditch beside it, the bare elm twigs outside the bathroom window. The sun shines sideways at the house, brilliantly, impartially. Seeing it through the kitchen window when she comes down to make breakfast, Erica Tate feels her emotional temperature, which has been unnaturally low of late, rise several degrees.

'Tomorrow's the beginning of spring,' she says to Jeffrey Tate, aged fifteen, as he stumbles into the room fastening his shirt.

'What's for breakfast?'

'Eggs, toast, jam –'

'Any sausages?'

'No, not today.' Erica tries to keep her voice cheerful.

'There's never anything to eat in this house,' Jeffrey complains, falling heavily into his chair.

Suppressing several possible answers to this remark, Erica sets a plate before her son and turns towards the stairs. 'Matilda! It's twenty minutes to eight.'

'All right! I heard you the first time.'

'Look at that sun,' Erica says to her daughter a few minutes later. 'Tomorrow's the first day of spring.'

No reply. Erica sets a plate in front of Matilda, who will be thirteen next month.

'I can't eat this stuff. It's fattening.'

'It's not fattening, it's just an ordinary breakfast, eggs, toast – Anyhow, you're not fat.'

'Everything has gobs of butter on it. It's all soaked in grease.'

'Aw, shut up, Muffy, you'll make me barf.'

Again Erica suppresses several rejoinders. 'Would you like me to make you a piece of toast without butter?' she asks rather thinly.

'Okay. If you can do it fast.'

The sun continues to shine into the kitchen. Standing by the toaster, Erica contemplates her children, whom she once thought were the most beautiful beings on earth. Jeffrey's streaked blond hair hangs tangled and unwashed over his eyes in front and his collar in back; he hunches awkwardly above the table, cramming fried egg into his mouth and chewing noisily. Matilda, who is wearing a peevish expression and an orange tie-dyed jersey which looks as if it had been spat on, is stripping the crusts off her toast with her fingers. Chomp, crunch, scratch.

The noises sound loud in Erica's head; louder still, as if amplified: CHOMP, CRUNCH, SCRATCH – No. That is coming from outside. She goes to the window. In the field beyond the orchard, something yellow is moving.

'Hey, the bulldozer's back,' Jeffrey exclaims.

'I guess they're going to put up another ranch-house,' his sister says.

The tone of both these remarks is neutral, even conversational; yet they strike Erica as more coarse and cold than anything that has yet been said this morning. 'You don't care what's happening to our road!' she cries. 'How can you be so selfish, so unfeeling? You don't really mind at all, either of you!'

Her children go on eating. It is evident that they do not.

Chomp; smash. The hands of the clock over the sink move towards eight. Jeffrey and Matilda rise, grumbling, grab their coats and books, and leave to catch the bus for junior high. Alone in the kitchen, Erica clears the table. She pours herself a cup of coffee, puts the buttered toast Matilda refused on a clean plate, and sits down. She starts to reach for the sugar bowl, and stops. Then she puts her head down on the table beside a splash of milk and some blobs of cherry jam, and weeps painfully. Tears run sideways across her small, slightly worn, delicate features, and into her crisp dark hair.

Read the extract again closely, and prepare from it a script suitable for television. You will find some aspects easy to incorporate, but others may have to be adapted or left out altogether. Here is a plan of the set:

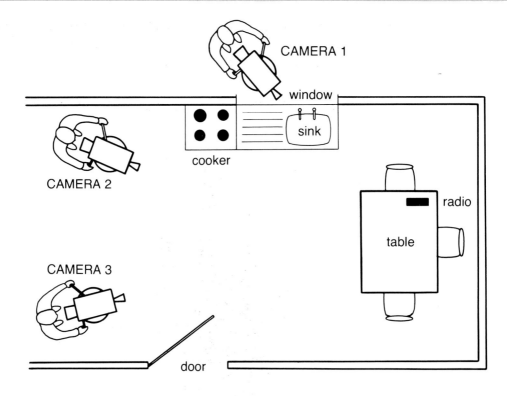

In a television studio the director will be able to use several cameras during the performance. The camera script shows the individual shots and where the cuts between cameras happen. Here is the script for the opening of the scene:

CAMERA No	TYPE OF SHOT	DIALOGUE	DIRECTIONS
1	Close up of Erica's face, zoom out to reveal Jeffrey.		Erica is at the sink, smiling slightly as she washes up. Summer music on the radio. Sound of feet clomping downstairs. Erica frowns then fixes her smile back on. Enter Jeffrey behind her.
3	long shot		Jeffrey stumbles in, fastening his shirt. Turns off radio, sits down.
2	close up of Erica	*ERICA*: (breezily) Tomorrow's the beginning of Spring.	She looks out of the window.
3	mid shot of Jeffrey	*JEFFREY*: (rudely) What's for breakfast?	

Continue writing the script into the columns in sufficient detail for the director, actors and camera operators to make the video in your absence. You will find the following diagram useful for describing the type of shot you want:

Afterwards . . .

Make a list of the problems you encountered in adapting the passage for television, and how you dealt with them.

Make another list of the things you found easy to adapt.

Notice that television is a very good medium for dialogue and for showing immediate reactions: it is less suitable for showing private thought or detailed accounts of feelings and memories.

TRY IT YOURSELF

Below is a second passage about Erica in which you face further difficulties which require imaginative solutions.

Jeffrey will be living at home for nearly four more years. Matilda will be with them for nearly six more years. As Erica is contemplating these facts, with her head on the damp table, the telephone rings.

She sits up, rubs her eyes dry, and answers.

'Hello, this is Helen in the Political Science Office, how are you today? . . . Oh, I'm very well too . . . There's a letter here, for Brian, it's marked URGENT PERSONAL, and I wondered . . . Well if he's going to call you tonight, that's fine . . . That's a good idea. I'll phone Mrs Zimmern in the French Department now and ask her to pick it up . . . You're welcome.'

This conversation, though banal, raises Erica's morale. It reminds her that she is successfully married, whereas Helen is a widow, and her best friend Danielle Zimmern a divorcee; that Brian is an important professor who receives urgent business letters; and that he calls home every evening when he is out of town.

She is encouraged to stand up, to clear the table and do the dishes and start her day's work. She picks up the house, skipping the children's rooms; washes out two sweaters; draws for an hour and a half; and makes herself a chicken sandwich. After lunch she goes shopping and to the bank, driving cautiously, for the sky has darkened again and an icy drizzle is falling from it. Her morale has fallen also, and a parody of Auden, composed by her friend Danielle some years ago, keeps running tediously in her head:

> Cleopatra's lips are kissed
> while an unimportant wife
> writes 'I do not like my life'
> underneath her shopping list.

She drives home, puts away the groceries, makes a raspberrry mousse, and is mixing some lemon cookies when Danielle's VW pulls into the driveway.

'What a hell of a day, huh? Spring, it says on the calendar . . . Oh, here's that letter for Brian, before I forget,' Danielle says, stepping out of her slushy boots on the back porch and coming into the kitchen in purple tights.

'Thank you. How is everything?' Erica puts the letter on a shelf in front of cookbooks without looking at it. 'Would you like some coffee?'

'Love it. The kids won't be home till four, thank God.' Danielle pulls off her coat with the careless, angry energy that has lately marked all of her actions, and flings it towards a chair. Twenty years ago, when Erica first met her, she had a similar energy – only then it was not angry, but joyful.

Erica and Danielle had known each other at college, though not intimately – Danielle being a year ahead, and in a different set. After graduation they had lost touch; in the autumn of 1964, when Danielle's husband joined the English Department and the family moved to Corinth, Erica was not aware of it; nor did Danielle realise that Erica already lived there. But a few weeks after their accidental meeting at Atwater's Supermarket, each accompanied by a nine-year-old daughter, it was as if they had remained friends uninterruptedly.

Danielle, like Erica, has been described by her admirers as tall, dark-haired, and beautiful. But where Erica is narrow, in the shoulders and hips, Danielle is broad; she is deep-bosomed, and stands on sturdy baroque legs. Her hair is long, heavy, and straight, with a russet overtone; her skin has a russet glow even in the northern winter, when Erica bleaches to the colour of cream. People who do not much like Erica admit that she is pretty, while those (a larger number) who do not much like Danielle admit that she is good-looking.

Discuss the problems which face the scriptwriter and how you would solve them. What would you leave out, change or communicate in a different way?

Do not write a detailed camera script, but decide how many small scenes you would need to televise the passage. Record your answer in the form of a list of scenes.

Afterwards . . .

Write a report for your teacher on the problems of adapting prose for television, based on your experience of preparing scripts from these passages. It is easier to make points by discussing particular examples.

PRACTICAL ASSIGNMENT

In this assignment, you prepare a short script for a classroom video. Your classroom is a ready-made set and you will not have the problems of adapting ideas from prose. You can start from scratch in ideal conditions, and tailor-make the script to suit yourself.

It all sounds so easy . . . but is it?

Take note as you prepare for this recording how much you have to consider, even in a custom-made video.

1 The play is set in a classroom and features five to seven students, a teacher and a headteacher or principal. Prepare one corner of your classroom as the set:

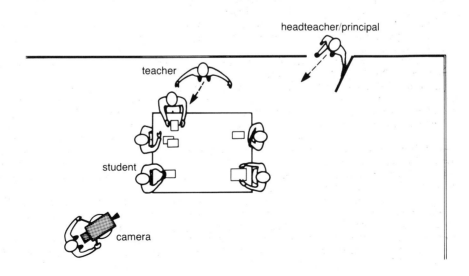

2 Work out some ideas for a script based on the following scenario:

- Teacher collecting in homework
- Assorted excuses for lack of homework
- One student explains how family dog has eaten the homework (the only student telling the truth!)
- General amusement at thin excuse
- Teacher's response
- Enter headteacher/principal

Conclude the scene as you wish . . .

3 Write a full script. You can improvise first and write afterwards, or write first and then act out. Your completed scripts must include dialogue, stage directions and camera instructions like those in the sample script above.

4 Hold a rehearsal. Check that there are no obstructions in the way of the camera, and decide where to stop and start the recording so that the camera operator can change position and focus. It is also easier for the actors if the recording is broken into short sections, because parts are easier to remember. View each shot on the instant playback and deal with mistakes by re-recording the shot before you continue.

Afterwards . . .

First, report in writing the major difficulties you encountered in getting this sketch onto video. You should include all aspects of the recording such as practical problems, technical hitches and team organisation.

Secondly, how adequate did you find the script? You can judge this by asking another group to reproduce your sketch by following your script without the benefit of discussion with the writers. Take note that professional script writers hand over responsibility in the same way to their producers and directors. They can't assume that their intentions are obvious; if there are things they want to appear in the programme they must be spelt out in the script.

Out of the Can

INTRODUCTION

Once all the shots have been recorded, the videotape is ready for editing. The director looks over the material and asks the editor to piece together the chosen shots in a particular order. They can:

- choose between alternative shots
- cut bits out
- put them back in
- change the order of shots
- change the sounds
- add in new sounds
- link the shots in different ways
- incorporate special effects

The videotape itself holds the pictures as a magnetic signal. Unlike film which is edited by hand, all videotape is edited electronically by transferring material from one machine to another. The tape is never touched.

The director and editor work in an edit suite, choosing shots and seeing the effect on screen before they make a final choice. If they are satisfied with it, they include it in the programme. As they work, they compile a programme tape of the chosen shots.

/ A Videotape Edit Suite

TRY IT YOURSELF

Look closely at the following 24 pictures. Each one represents a moving television picture, lasting just a few moments. Choose any ten of them placed in any order to tell a story. Split into groups, each group trying to tell a different story:

- a comic story   - a suspense thriller
- a romantic story   - an all-action adventure

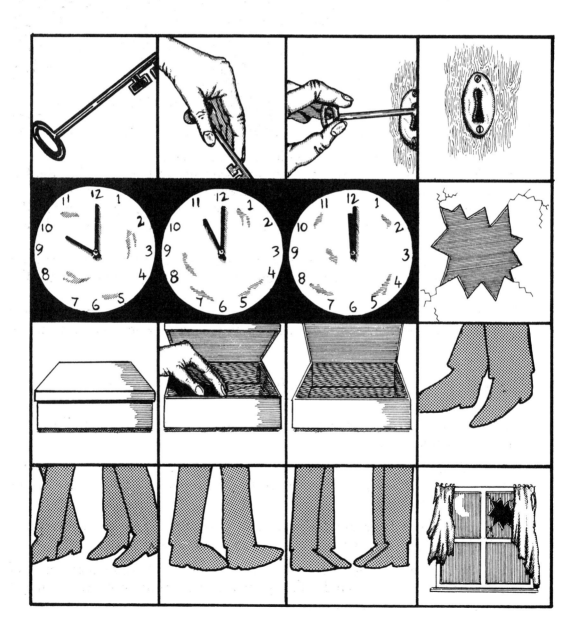

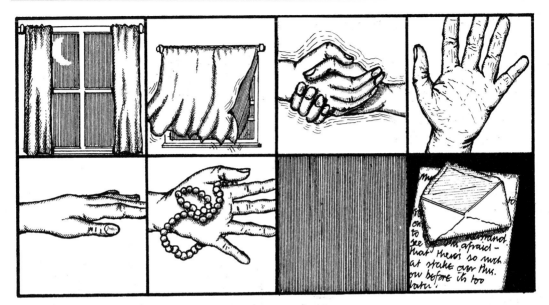

Put your photocopies of the ten pictures in the chosen order.

Ask someone outside the group to 'read' your sequence and say what they think is happening in it. Notice the difference between their interpretation and your intention.

Now provide a title of no more than five words, and ask a different person outside the group to read the sequence and interpret it. How far has the title influenced their interpretation of the pictures?

Finally, write a brief soundtrack of dialogue and sound effects only, to go with each picture. Now see if a reader outside the group understands the pictures in exactly the way you do.

Look how other groups have used the pictures you chose. Find examples to show that the same picture can have a different meaning depending on its context and the soundtrack.

PRACTICAL ASSIGNMENT

Prepare two short videos which present opposing views of your school or college – one flattering, one unflattering.

1 First of all make a list of all the places and activities which create a good impression, such as students working in a pleasant corner of the library or reading on the grass one sunny lunch hour.

2 Make another list of images which would give a less flattering impression, such as the boiler house on a wet afternoon, or graffiti on loo doors.

3 Choose an appropriate piece of music to accompany each tape, such as a piece of classical music or a pop record with appropriate lyrics. Your music teacher might make suggestions and loan records.

4 Select about one minute of your music and plan the order of shots to fit into the time available. It can be useful knowing your music in advance, so that you can match the shots to suit the music. Precise timing is difficult, but you can keep track by using an audio cassette at the same time as the video playback.

5 Watch the video and write a report on it for the teacher, to include comments about:

- general reactions
- suitability of images
- suitability of music
- technical quality
- artistic quality
- strong points
- suggestions for improvement

VIEWING ASSIGNMENT

Watch out for a party political broadcast. Notice how it presents a positive and pleasing image of the party's own policies. Discuss what use it makes of:

- the issues selected for discussion
- images of their policies at work (e.g. in health, education or industry)
- images of other people's policies at work
- the background setting of the speaker
- the mood suggested by the music
- the choice of speakers

It can also be revealing to consider:

- which policies are not discussed – and why not
- who is not invited to speak – and why not
- what pictures they might have used – but did not

Remember that it is the right of a political party to present a positive image of itself and that airtime is very short for complex political arguments. Moreover, a political broadcast never pretends to be anything else: it is quite open about the way it wants to influence the audience. Reserve some suspicion for the programmes which claim to be neutral or balanced or even above politics, because we cannot tell simply by looking what was cut and what was never recorded. Bias of this sort is harder to detect.

Coming Soon

INTRODUCTION

Viewers are encouraged to watch programmes by advance publicity such as previews and 'trailer' promotions. In promoting a programme, many compromises must be made to select material which is both representative and brief to excite interest without giving too much away.

PREVIEWS

Previews are written by critics who have seen programmes in advance. The television companies invite them in to view their forthcoming attractions, and the critic then writes a brief introduction to the programme for the viewers. The idea is that it helps viewers to select their evening's viewing. Not every programme is released in advance this way, and most newspapers and magazines only offer a few lines for previews. In this short space, the critic must provide a useful introduction without spoiling any surprises and without making up people's minds for them.

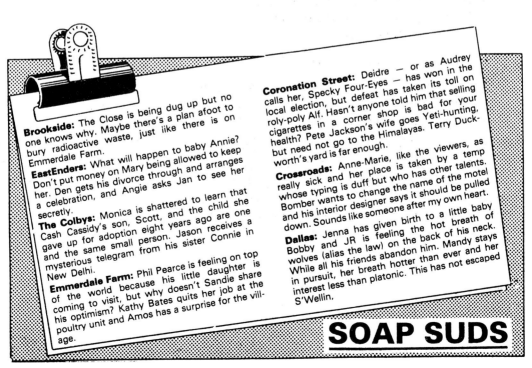

Brookside: The Close is being dug up but no one knows why. Maybe there's a plan afoot to bury radioactive waste, just like there is on Emmerdale Farm.

EastEnders: What will happen to baby Annie? Don't put money on Mary being allowed to keep her. Den gets his divorce through and arranges a celebration, and Angie asks Jan to see her secretly.

The Colbys: Monica is shattered to learn that Cash Cassidy's son, Scott, and the child she gave up for adoption eight years ago are one and the same small person. Jason receives a mysterious telegram from his sister Connie in New Delhi.

Emmerdale Farm: Phil Pearce is feeling on top of the world because his little daughter is coming to visit, but why doesn't Sandie share his optimism? Kathy Bates quits her job at the poultry unit and Amos has a surprise for the village.

Coronation Street: Deidre — or as Audrey calls her, Specky Four-Eyes — has won in the local election, but defeat has taken its toll on roly-poly Alf. Hasn't anyone told him that selling cigarettes in a corner shop is bad for your health? Pete Jackson's wife goes Yeti-hunting, but need not go to the Himalayas. Terry Duckworth's yard is far enough.

Crossroads: Anne-Marie, like the viewers, as really sick and her place is taken by a temp whose typing is duff but who has other talents. Bomber wants to change the name of the motel and his interior designer says it should be pulled down. Sounds like someone after my own heart.

Dallas: Jenna has given birth to a little baby Bobby and JR is feeling the hot breath of wolves (alias the law) on the back of his neck. While all his friends abandon him. Mandy stays in pursuit, her breath hotter than ever and her interest less than platonic. This has not escaped S'Wellin.

SOAP SUDS

2.00 **CARE BEARS :** Cartoon.
2.30 **INTERNATIONAL ATHLETICS :** The Kodak AAA Championships from Crystal Palace. This is the final selection meeting before the World Championship in Rome. Taking part are Steve Cram, Steve Ovett, Colin Jackson and Roger Black.
*4.30 **SHADOW OF THE STONE :** Children's serial stars Shirley Henderson as a girl possessed by a mystery.
5.00 **TURNING THE TIDE :** 'The Great Gene Robbery.' David Bellamy reveals a threat to the future of the ubiquitous potato.
5.30 **HAWAII FIVE-O :** ' A Bullet for McGarrett.' Students are hypnotised by a Chinese agent and instructed to commit murder.
6.30 **NEWS.**
6.40 **SING OUT :** Hymns and spirituals with Roger Whittaker, Gloria Gaynor and the St Anne's Cathedral Choir.
7.15 **TARBY'S FRAME GAME :** Game show hosted by Jimmy Tarbuck.
7.45 **WOLF TO THE SLAUGHTER :** Crime thriller in four parts based on a novel by Ruth Rendell. George Baker plays Detective Chief Inspector Wexford. His task is to find a murderer — and a corpse.
8.45 **NEWS.**
9.00 **CRAZY LIKE A FOX :** 'Fox in ¾ Time.' Harry's grandson's music teacher commits suicide. Or is it murder? Jack Warden and John Rubinstein star.
10.00 **WATCHING :** ' Leavings.' Brenda (Emma Wray) gets her marching orders from sister Pamela (Liza Tarbuck).
10.30 **THE JIMMY YOUNG TELEVISION PROGRAMME :** The moral issues surrounding Aids. Bishop Swing of California leads the debate. Followed by **LWT News Headlines.**
11.15 **THE UNDISPUTED WORLD HEAVYWEIGHT CHAMPIONSHIP :** A reprise of the Tyson/Tucker fight for those who did not catch the early morning programme.
12.15 **DERRICK :** German detective series. **Ends 1.15am.**
* Oracle subtitles.

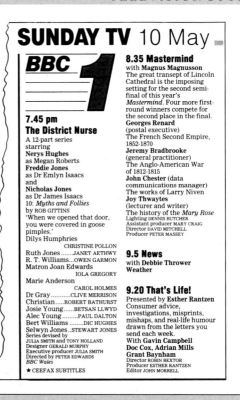

SUNDAY TV 10 May

BBC 1

7.45 pm
The District Nurse
A 12-part series starring
Nerys Hughes as Megan Roberts
Freddie Jones as Dr Emlyn Isaacs and
Nicholas Jones as Dr James Isaacs
10: *Myths and Follies* by ROB GITTINS
'When we opened that door, you were covered in goose pimples.'
Dilys Humphries
                          CHRISTINE POLLON
Ruth Jones ....JANET AETHWY
R. T. Williams...OWEN GARMON
Matron Joan Edwards
                              IOLA GREGORY
Marie Anderson
                         CAROL HOLMES
Dr Gray ....CLIVE MERRISON
Christian.....ROBERT BATHURST
Josie Young......BETSAN LLWYD
Alec Young.........PAUL DALTON
Bert Williams ....DIC HUGHES
Selwyn Jones ..STEWART JONES
Series devised by
JULIA SMITH and TONY HOLLAND
Designer GERALD MURPHY
Executive producer JULIA SMITH
Directed by PETER EDWARDS
BBC Wales
★ CEEFAX SUBTITLES

8.35 Mastermind
with **Magnus Magnusson**
The great transept of Lincoln Cathedral is the imposing setting for the second semifinal of this year's *Mastermind*. Four more firstround winners compete for the second place in the final.
Georges Renard
(postal executive)
The French Second Empire, 1852-1870
Jeremy Bradbrooke
(general practitioner)
The Anglo-American War of 1812-1815
John Chester (data communications manager)
The works of Larry Niven
Joy Thwaytes
(lecturer and writer)
The history of the *Mary Rose*
Lighting DENNIS BUTCHER
Assistant producer MARY CRAIG
Director DAVID MITCHELL
Producer PETER MASSEY

9.5 News
with **Debbie Thrower**
Weather

9.20 That's Life!
Presented by Esther Rantzen
Consumer advice, investigations, misprints, mishaps, and real-life humour drawn from the letters you send each week.
With **Gavin Campbell**
Doc Cox, Adrian Mills
Grant Baynham
Director ROBIN BEXTOR
Producer ESTHER RANTZEN
Editor JOHN MORRELL

Look over these previews and, bearing in mind the difficulties, discuss:

- what else you would like to hear about the programmes
- how useful you would find them in choosing your evening's viewing
- what compromises the previewers have made to deal with the limitations outlined above

PROMOTIONS

Promotions or 'trailers' offer the viewer a quick sample of future programmes. They pack a great deal of information into a few seconds, including the title and time of the programme and snatches of it to whet the appetite.

Watch one or two promotions, paying particular attention to the clips used. Why do you suppose these particular clips were selected from the programmes?

Here, **Steve White** explains how he goes about selecting material for a promotion:

What do you try to include in a promotion?
In a 30 second promotion I'd hope to include clips from several scenes, to feature the main stars, and to get across the flavour of the programme. Apart from the clips, the

information to get over is what the programme is called, when it's on, and on what channel, which is why promotions usually finish with the familiar captions showing that information. If it's a comedy, to actually get three short, easily-understood jokes into 30 seconds, as well as allowing for the announcer to say the time and day, is quite difficult. A promotion for Saturday night's viewing on ITV might have four programmes in it and last 45 seconds. Because you only have 10 or 15 seconds per programme there are a lot of things you simply can't fit in and you have to show just a glimpse, using an announcer's voice-over to describe the show rather than letting the clips speak for themselves.

How do you decide which programmes to promote?
Airtime for promotions is very tightly rationed, so priorities have to be made. A new programme that's not doing very well would be more strongly promoted than one that already has a large audience. Promotions are timed to reach certain audiences, so a game show, for example, would be promoted after a similar programme and not after, say, a late night drama.

How would you go about promoting a typical game show?
A game show usually has enough lively goings-on to make it fairly easy to promote. You might feature the prizes to be won, any celebrities taking part, and quick snatches of humour which suggest the atmosphere and excitement of the programme. Obviously you mustn't give away who wins, but you might show someone guessing the right answer during the game without making the end result obvious.

What about series and programmes with a story – a cop show for instance?
Cop shows are usually based on a particular character, so you'd use the cop as the selling point. I think people watch for the hero rather than the details of the plot, so I might have the star saying an amusing line even if it doesn't relate too much to this week's story, just to remind viewers of their favourite character.

Surely you want to include some action shots?
Some action scenes which are quite acceptable in context give a misleading impression of violence if they're used in isolation. You have to find a balance, to show the programme is lively and action-packed without putting people off with the false impression that it's a violent programme. Promotions are also seen at different times from the programmes they feature; a programme suitable for showing after 9 pm may be promoted at 7.30 pm. The audience then is different and you have to adjust the material to allow for that.

Steve White, promotions producer, LWT

Imagine you have the job of selecting clips for promotions. Make a list of the things you would look for in a clip from:

- a soap opera
- a football match
- an adventure film
- a debate between the Prime Minister and the Leader of the Opposition
- a rock concert
- a situation comedy

TRY IT YOURSELF

Here is a list of clips taken from next Saturday evening's programmes. There is only time in one promotion to feature *three* programmes, each one containing *three* clips.

Clips Available for Promotions

AMERICAN COP PROGRAMME
a crime being committed
car chase
shoot-out
desperate telephone call
punch-up

ACTION MOVIE
car chase
shoot-out
dramatic escape
punch-up
romantic scene

GAME SHOW
the big prize
the host talking to a contestant
a funny moment
a tense moment, lots of money at stake
the host's assistant

NEWS
title sequence
pictures from the main story
tough question during an important interview
dramatic pictures of a lifeboat rescue
pictures from Buckingham Palace – royal baby

VARIETY SHOW
the star turn
the host waving
big dance number
a dynamic but unknown new group
a funny moment

LATE NIGHT MOVIE
romantic scene
another romantic scene
an argument
a sad parting
an aeroplane taking off
an aeroplane landing

Prepare two promotions: one to be transmitted at 10 pm on Friday, and another to be transmitted at 5 pm on Saturday afternoon. You may re-use material where it is appropriate.

Bearing in mind the two different audiences, compile a list showing which programmes you will feature, which clips you will include and the order in which you will use them.

Write the voice-over which will accompany them, and suggest what sort of music, if any, you will use. Put this on tape if possible, making up any programme dialogue you need.

When you have completed this activity, discuss briefly the factors which influenced your choice and presentation of the material.

A BRIEF HISTORY OF BRITISH TELEVISION

How much do you know about the history of television? Test yourself by putting this list of facts and events into the order in which they happened.

FIRST EPISODE OF *CORONATION STREET*
1 MILLION TV SETS IN THE UK
5 MILLION TV SETS IN THE UK
19 MILLION TV SETS IN THE UK
BREAKFAST TELEVISION LAUNCHED
FALKLANDS WAR
BBC2 LAUNCHED
OFFICIAL LAUNCH OF COLOUR TELEVISION
FIRST EPISODE OF *EASTENDERS*
THE WEDDING OF PRINCESS ANNE
FIRST REGULAR NEWS BULLETIN
THE SHOOTING OF JR
THE CORONATION OF QUEEN ELIZABETH II
FIRST REGULAR TELEVISION SERVICE (BBC1)
FIRST VIDEO-RECORDED PROGRAMME SHOWN
ENGLAND WON THE WORLD CUP
CHANNEL 4 LAUNCHED
FIRST SCREENING OF *TOP OF THE POPS*
THE WEDDING OF CHARLES AND DIANA
FIRST SATELLITE PICTURES FROM AMERICA
LIVE PICTURES OF THE FIRST MOON LANDING
ITV LAUNCHED

Afterwards you can check against a list of dates on page 96.

IN THE BEGINNING

Although the BBC began broadcasting before the Second World War, very few households could afford sets and the transmitters did not cover the whole country. After the War, improving standards of living meant that more people could afford sets, and programmes were adjusted to appeal to a mass audience. What started out as a

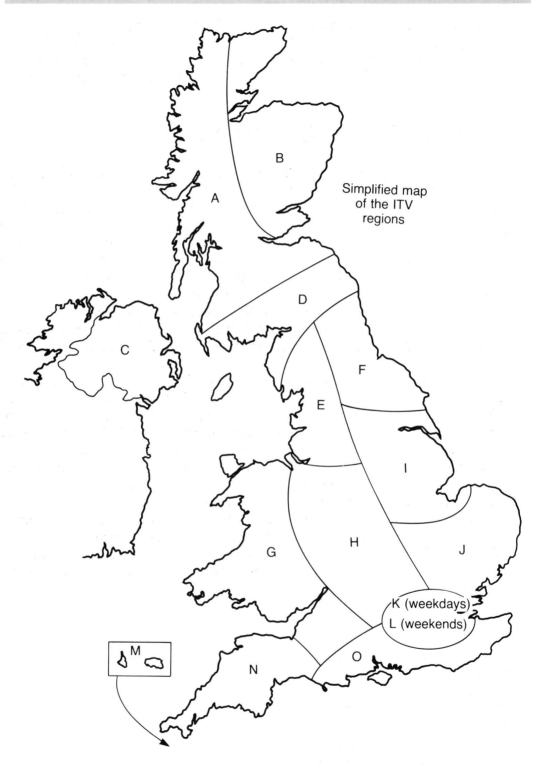

Simplified map
of the ITV
regions

limited public service run by the BBC for a privileged few became a popular part of everyday life for millions. Up to 1955 there was just one channel, the BBC, and everyone who used a television set in their home had to pay a certain amount towards the cost of the service. They still do. Find out how much the licence costs today.

COMMERCIAL TELEVISION

In 1954, the government decided to set up a second service to be run by privately-owned companies. This service was called Independent Television, although neither the ITV nor the BBC is 'independent' of government and financial restraints. It is perhaps more accurate to think of it as commercial television; in other words, it is run for profit which is made by selling airtime to advertisers in the commercial breaks.

The country was divided up into regions, and television companies competed for the right to broadcast in each one. The franchise – the right to broadcast – was given to the companies which promised the best service and which could meet the guidelines set down, such as how many programmes had to be made, how the station had to offer programmes of local interest, and how much it could import from other countries. These rules are decided and checked by the Independent Broadcasting Authority (the IBA).

At first, companies were slow to come forward in what seemed like a risky new venture. But it soon became obvious that commercial television was a money spinner. Advertisers realised that there was a huge captive audience sitting in their own living-rooms, who could afford television sets and could probably afford their products too. If they could be kept in their seats during the breaks – not off to the bathroom or the kitchen – they might be persuaded to become customers. Advertisements have to be entertaining to keep the attention of the audience, like ingenious miniature programmes popped in between the scheduled ones.

Since the start of ITV, the franchises have been renewed and the areas changed on several occasions. In 1983, a further franchise was added with the introduction of national breakfast-time commercial television. This was won by TV-am. Opposite is a map of the ITV areas as they stand today. Can you match each area to one of the stations below?

ANGLIA	LWT
BORDER	STV
CENTRAL	THAMES
CHANNEL	TSW
GRAMPIAN	TVS
GRANADA	TYNE-TEES
HTV (WALES) (WEST)	ULSTER
	YORKSHIRE

Afterwards, check your answers against the map on p. 97.

The franchise is renewed every few years and the companies have to compete once more for the right to broadcast. Occasionally, the IBA rejects an existing company and appoints a new one, but this is quite rare.

BBC2 AND CHANNEL 4

The BBC expanded in 1964 with the launch of BBC2. The intention was to provide a fresh, alternative service but the channel soon gained a reputation as being highbrow and specialised. Since then it has become popular for its high-quality and in-depth programmes. ITV also expanded in 1982 by opening a new channel – Channel 4. One of its aims was to provide programmes for minority groups in society who were under-represented on the existing channels. Whereas BBC2 is financed along with BBC1 by the TV licence, Channel 4 is financed by the other ITV companies who pay a levy – a sum of money which depends upon the size of their income. In return, the companies keep the money made from the sale of advertising airtime on Channel 4. Channel 4 does not make its own programmes, but commissions them from other companies. The credits at the end of Channel 4 programmes reveal where they were made.

TECHNOLOGY

Advances in technology influence television programmes. Snooker programmes were made possible by the invention of colour television, for example, and this drew big new audiences to the game. Snooker is big business now. At the same time, television itself has stimulated new technology. The videotape recorder was developed in America so that the western states, whose day begins several hours later than the eastern states, could witness the news and events which were viewed live in the east.

In the last few years, new technology has allowed satellite transmission of programmes across the world, and in the near future cable and satellite services will be received in many homes. This could mean dozens of channels to choose from, but not necessarily more or better programmes. Operators of future services will be tempted to cut back on technical standards and to buy in cheap shows rather than incur the high costs of making their own programmes.

IDENTITY

Because there are four channels competing for viewers, each one strives to create an identity or an image which the viewer will find pleasing. Each station advertises itself hoping that its name, tune or image will stick in the mind and encourage the viewer to tune in again.

One important way of creating an identity is the use of a station *logo* such as these:

Study each logo carefully and decide what it tries to tell you about the station. Can you remember the music which goes with each logo? Can you draw a colour copy of each one? Can you recall how each logo appears to move on the screen?

Even individual programmes create an image for themselves, in their title sequences and theme tunes.

Get into teams. Find ten programme titles and challenge another team to hum or sing the theme tune to each one. For the second round of the quiz, take ten television theme tunes and get the other team to identify the programmes.

Which theme tunes were the best-known and most popular? These are the ones which stick in the mind and help the viewer to identify the programme. Choose your own three favourites and explain to someone else why they seem especially appropriate and successful.

Title sequences are the sounds and pictures which open a programme. It is easy to remember theme music, but difficult to remember opening pictures. Test this out by trying to recall the opening pictures which accompany the theme tunes you used earlier for the quiz.

Study the opening sequences from different types of programme:

e.g.　a quiz
　　　a drama
　　　the news
　　　an American soap opera
　　　a science programme

Use the pause or slow-motion button to observe the pictures in detail. For each programme, answer the following questions:

1　Explain the name of the programme.

2　What hints are there in the pictures about the programme which will follow?

3　Find a few words which would describe the music as well as the pictures – this should pinpoint the image the programme wishes to have.

4　What differences do you notice between British and American title sequences?

TRY IT YOURSELF

You are a designer who has received the following challenge:

ISLAND TELEVISION COMPETITION
!!!!

Designers are invited to submit material in a competition to create an identity for this brand new television station and its programmes. The winner will win a permanent contract and a fabulous salary. The new station will serve islands off the coast of Britain.

Competitors must submit the following design ideas:

A name and logo for the new station

A title for
— a quiz show based on island history and local knowledge.

— a series about the history of voyages

— a comedy based on characters and events in a large supermarket

Title sequences for — a programme on local politics

— a science programme about the sea

Submissions may take the form of sketches, tape recordings, video tapes, written descriptions or computer graphics. The judges are looking for original and appropriate designs which will grab the attention whilst providing the viewer with an honest impression of the station and its programmes.

Either as an individual or in groups, prepare your entry and submit it to the teacher.

ANSWERS

List of Dates

1932 FIRST REGULAR TELEVISION SERVICE
(BBC1)
There were four programmes a week,
broadcast between 11–11.30 pm. In the
first programme, Louie Freear sang 'I
Want To Be A Lady'.

1948 FIRST REGULAR NEWS BULLETIN
A twice-weekly 15-minute bulletin in
sound only, with occasional still pictures.
The first stories were about high meat
prices (meat had been rationed during
the War) and a truce in Indo-China. In
1955 Richard Baker and Kenneth
Kendall became the first newsreaders to
be seen on screen. More and more
pictures appeared in the bulletins – an
'illustrated summary', as it was called.

1951 1 MILLION TV SETS IN THE UK
The licence fee cost £2. In the same year,
the first television detector vans moved
into action.

1953 THE CORONATION OF QUEEN
ELIZABETH II
This event was shown on television, and
accounts for the huge number of people
who bought television sets at this time.

1955 5 MILLION TV SETS IN THE UK
The licence fee cost £3.

1955 ITV LAUNCHED
The first programme showed the
speeches at a special dinner in London
which launched the service.

1958 FIRST RECORDED PROGRAMME SHOWN
Panorama on BBC1.

1960 FIRST EPISODE OF *CORONATION
STREET*
The world's longest-running serial, it
dominated the ratings until the coming of
EastEnders.

1962 FIRST SATELLITE PICTURES FROM
AMERICA
The Telstar satellite broadcast 18
minutes of pictures – including a rocket
site, a press conference with the
President and part of a baseball game.
After 18 minutes, the satellite moved out
of range. Later satellites move with the
earth and are always in range above the
Atlantic.

1964 FIRST SCREENING OF *TOP OF THE POPS*
New Year's Day. Jimmy Savile was the
DJ and his guests included the Rolling
Stones, Dusty Springfield, the Dave Clark
Five, the Hollies and the Swinging Blue
Jeans.

1964 BBC2 LAUNCHED

1966 ENGLAND WON THE WORLD CUP
England won 4–2 (in extra time).
Thirty-two million watched. There were
no action replays; they started in 1968
for a cricket match.

1967 OFFICIAL LAUNCH OF COLOUR
TELEVISION
Seven hours of colour television hit the
screens on 1 July – mainly tennis from
Wimbledon.

1969 LIVE PICTURES OF THE FIRST MOON
LANDING
723 million viewers worldwide saw Neil
Armstrong put his foot on the moon.
David Frost presented the ITV
programme. His guests included Cilla
Black, Dame Sybil Thorndike and the
singer Engelbert Humperdinck.

1973 THE WEDDING OF PRINCESS ANNE
The first royal wedding in colour. Only 25
per cent of sets were colour, but the
wedding had a big impact on sales.

1980   THE SHOOTING OF JR
Who shot JR in the soap opera *Dallas*?
Kristen did. The question made
newspaper headlines and the news
bulletins. *Dallas* fever died down after
people found the answer.

1981   19 MILLION TV SETS IN THE UK
Licence fees cost £15 for black and white
sets, £46 for colour.

1981   THE WEDDING OF CHARLES AND
DIANA
The biggest audience in the world (750
million) watched it, a record 39 million of
them in Britain. It was the biggest outside
broadcast ever. There was a surge in
sales of video recorders. The previous
record audience in Britain was the 1970
World Cup game between Brazil and
England.

1982   CHANNEL 4 LAUNCHED

1982   FALKLANDS WAR
Notable for how little was seen on
television. News was carefully restricted
to a handful of deadpan summaries
issued by the Ministry of Defence.

1983   BREAKFAST TELEVISION LAUNCHED
The BBC *Breakfast Time* programme
lasted two and a half hours and was
hosted by Frank Bough and Selina Scott.
Their guests included Sir Harry Secombe.

1985   FIRST EPISODE OF *EASTENDERS*
The programme dislodged *Coronation
Street* from the top of the ratings. Up to
25 million people watch it every week.

Map of ITV Regions

PART THREE / *Responding to Television*

With a television in nearly every home, it is only right to be worried about its effects on viewers. From eye strain to daredevil copycat stunts, there is concern about every aspect of viewing. In particular we fear the viewer who has turned into a television zombie collapsed in an armchair before the set, having lost interest in the 'real' world and become a slave to the fantasy one. Most particularly, we fear that this zombie is a young zombie.

Does this television zombie exist? Are young people really hooked on television, except for brief excursions into the real world to recreate the death-defying antics of their heroes? Most unlikely. Though we appear absorbed in our viewing, and passive in the presence of a television screen, our brains are in fact very active in making sense of the sounds and pictures as they go along, piecing together the story. We 'read' television like a book, and we are often critical. Indeed, discussing television programmes is almost a national pastime. Every day programmes are previewed and reviewed, discussed, ignored, laughed at, recorded, and even . . . switched off.

The effects of television are not dramatic or obvious. They are subtle. The way it decides what is news and what is not, what is worth showing and what is not, what is balanced and what is not, what is funny and what is not – these are the things that affect the way we look at the world, because they seem normal and acceptable. Countrywide, television is something we share – it is part of our heritage now.

Something which plays such a large part in everyday life is worth thinking about. The way television is organised and the way decisions are taken influences the programmes which are made and the values they encourage. In this section, we look at the way viewers respond to television at a personal level, and at a wider social level, and consider some of the longer-term issues which face us.

Personal Responses

PRIVATE VIEWING JOURNALS

A viewing journal is a diary of personal thoughts about the programmes you watch on television. Why keep one? First, it will encourage you to look more critically at your favourite programmes. Secondly, writing down your ideas will help you to pin down exactly what you mean. And thirdly, you will have some ideas worked out for discussion later.

One of the problems about viewing journals is when to write them. Some people like to write them after the programme, so that they can watch it uninterrupted. This means you have to remember quite a lot. Other people prefer to keep notes as they watch. This can be useful for focusing the attention and picking up reactions as they flash through the mind at the time. A good compromise is to jot down some key points about the programme as you watch it – just a word or two to remind you later – and then spend a few minutes afterwards filling them out.

Here are some examples:

```
            LAST  8  MINUTES  OF     GARDENER'S  DIRECT  LINE  (BBC1)

LIFTING ONIONS   — 'sprout net' useful
OUT OF GROUND      dry off
                   don't bend necks    } useful tips
                   use thick necks first

                 — awful set! — can't see plants in the
                   ground.

PHONE - IN       — good quality sound - a bit awkward
CALLERS' QUESTIONS  waiting for callers to finish — just
                   stand around.
                 ⚹ Who are they talking to? camera?
                   chairperson? a bit confusing
                 — awkward chairperson — not paying a lot
                   of attention, glancing at notes + lists.
                 — how do they have eg's ready in studio
                   if the calls are live??
                 — strange mix of callers — one absurd
                   one, really embarrassing.

EG'S OF          — useful to SEE eg's - better than drawings
FUNGUS             + photos   eg 'club root' disease
                 — but difficult to catch the Latin names
                   + weedkiller names — these better in print

ADVICE   — common sense — 3 people chatting (host,
           chair + guest) — more like a friendly
           get together — rather bitty — unusual local
           accents — seasonal advice.
```

BRASS TACKS.

This programme set out to probe the news media. To ask — how & why news stories are selected
— whose interests journalists serve
— how standards of taste and decency are decided.

I felt disappointed and irritated by it. 'Brass Tacks' suggests getting down to the nitty-gritty, an in-depth discussion. Instead we got a quick-fire barrage of one-liners. The format of a panel of 'experts' + a selected audience was to blame. Presenter lobbed questions back and forth but didn't pause to consider any of the answers. Why couldn't we have a detailed discussion of just one of the points raised, instead of this relentless sparring match?

It has left my nerves frayed and made me feel powerless. This programme shows, ironically, a weakness of television – the love of sensation. Instead of the promised debate it staged a slanging match – more entertainment than education.

NEWS
9.45
SUNDAY
6th SEP

TITLES — FAMILIAR MUSIC. SHORT. NO PICTURES
'COS SUNDAY'?

APPETISERS — HEADLINES — ALL PEOPLE — SCARGILL
IN PICTURES — PRINCE WILLIAM
— PARTY LEADERS

ALL SCARGILL
SCARGILL SAID THIS, — MINERS OVERTIME
SAID THAT OBSESSED BAN – NEW WORKING — WORDS 'BUST UP', 'CLIMB DOWN'
WITH SCARGILL CONDITIONS 'GO-AHEAD' V. COLLOQUIAL
TALKS DOWN, MAKING IT SIMPLE
ALL ABOUT THE
BAN, NOT THE LIBERAL/ SDP MERGER — LOTS OF PICTURES OF PRESS MEN
CAUSE ALL PICS TAKING PICTURES! A 'PHOTO-
NO STORY! ↓ OPPORTUNITY' YAWN
ABOUT THEIR AGE MURDERS – COUPLE
IS IT REALLY WORSE OVER 80
IF YOU'RE OLD? IT'S SMOTHERED — WHY MENTION HIS ARTHRITIS?
JUST AS BAD KILLING — MOTIVE?? NOT WEALTHY. BURGLED
YOUNG PEOPLE?! ↓ WEEK BEFORE.

ATTACK ON CHAUFFEUR — ?? MPS DRIVER – IRELAND?
↓
SIEGE — WIFE HOSTAGE
LATE & BRIEF 3RD DAY – 1st I'VE HEARD OF IT
–UNUSUAL; IT'S BEEN GULF CRISIS — NO PICS
HEADLINES SO FAR. ↓
WAR IN CHAD
WHY ARE THEY ATTACK ON LIBYA — TOO QUICK WHY?? NEVER
AT WAR? (I NEVER EXPLAINS WHY?) V FRUSTRATING
KNEW) MAP ONLY WHY?
MACABRE MOTORWAY PILE-UP — INTERVIEWING SURVIVORS
↓ — HAPPENED YESTERDAY! BIT
LINKED TO LATE
ATTACK ON CHAUFFEUR SECURITY AT BALMORAL — JUST AN EXCUSE TO SHOW
– 'TERRORIST THREAT' PICS OF PRINCE WILLIAM
— SAME PICTURE, DIFFERENT ANGLE
USUAL WINNING-LINE GOLD MEDAL — FATIMA WHITBREAD CHEEKY!
SHOTS. (ATHLETICS) JAVELIN 'THE GOLDEN TOUCH'
↓ CRAM 8TH - REALLY OTT 'TOTAL
HUMILIATION', 'BROKEN HIMSELF', ETC
GRAND PRIX
↓ YAWN!
CRICKET

WRITING REVIEWS

Viewing journals are personal, but reviews are written for other people. You can find examples of reviews in newspapers and magazines. What is the point of writing a review?

- To express a point of view
- To think through reasons for liking or disliking a programme
- To put a programme into perspective, to judge its value and significance
- To influence and educate the opinions of the reader
- To entertain and interest the reader

Here are some extracts from reviews about television programmes:

Wimbledon week

According to the smart money, McEnroe's exit meant that Thursday's men's semi-final between Borg and Connors would be, in effect, the final. Alas, it was a dud match. Connors has run out of answers to what Dan calls 'the immaculate length of Borg'. Connors likes the ball to come at him in a straight line so that he can hit it back in another straight line. When it comes at him in a curve he uses up half his energy straightening it out again. Borg hits nothing but curves. Connors was left with little in the armoury except his new weapon, the Early Grunt.

As I revealed exclusively last week, Connors now grunts at the same time as he serves, instead of just afterwards. Since the grunt travels at the speed of sound, it arrives in the opponent's court marginally before the ball does. Ordinary opponents try to hit the grunt. Borg was not fooled. Indeed he quickly developed a Swedish counter-grunt. 'Hworf!' grunted Connors. 'Hwörjf!' grunted Borg. 'Game to Connors. Borg, rather,' cried the umpire helpfully. There they were, the two best: Connors with the long feet and the shoulders growing out of his ears, Borg looking like a hunch-backed, jut-bottomed version of Lizabeth Scott impersonating a bearded Apache princess. Back went Jimbo to the loneliness of the locker-room.

If Wmbldn was too much for your blood pressure there was always the punishing boredom of *International Athletics* (BBC1), piped to your living room from Malmö, Sweden. Obviously Borg has more reasons than tax avoidance for living in Monte Carlo. If Malmö is a typical Swedish metropolis, then it's a wonder the country has produced competitors in any events other than the 1,500 metres sleep-walk and the triple yawn. Could Britain qualify for the Europa Cup Final later in the year? To do so they would have to beat the Bulgarians.

Pattering around in front of the empty stands came a pack of runners, temporarily led by our man Coates. 'And Coates testing out the field,' said David Coleman. From that moment you knew Coates was doomed. 'The British team might have hoped that Coates might have put one or two more between himself and the Bulgarian.' Translated into English, this meant that Coates, on whom British Hopes had been Pinned, was on his way back to the loneliness of the locker-room. Nevertheless Britain qualified for the final.

CHARLIE'S ANGELS.
I.T.V. (Tuesdays 7.30 pm)

Yes, *Charlie's Angels* is a very badly made programme, costing over 330,000 dollars an episode to make – it has sloppy scripts, dull to inept camerawork, wooden acting, the whole works. As the producer says: "We're more concerned with hairdos and gowns than the twists and turns of the plot. . ." And ostensibly it's made to appeal to the same people that 'Pan's People' danced for, men who need some minimal excuse for ogling bare-legged women. Irredeemably *sexist*. But – captivated in spite of myself – I think it's both more interesting and more dangerous than, say, the Miss World contest. Charlie's Angels look pretty competent with their guns, and although they are not quick-witted they manage to out-manoeuvre the even dumber men around them. For all their bikinis, they come across as sexless – rather sporty and good fun, actually. I don't suppose the men who sit focused to their thighs notice, but it seems that the programme is also catering for an entirely different fantasy.

One 12 year old girl I talked to said she would like to be a Charlie's Angel when she grew up – because "They're glamorous *and* tough", and never fall for the men they lead on episode after episode. In real life we're all faced with a choice between being feminine, attractive and loved and being active and independent; but Charlie's Angels manage to do both. They are good at skiing, tennis, swimming, dancing, riding etc etc with not a curl out of place. They are a young girl's complete dream.

And that is what is sinister about this programme. In this 'liberated' world, girls might be dissatisfied with having to choose between being women and being people. So they are now told they don't have to make the choice. They can be beautiful and clever, they can have a husband and babies and be top brain surgeons – well, they can believe it until it's too late, and find that they are stuck where women have always been stuck.[. .]

Of course you can be liberated, it says – and now you'll all stop struggling and go home, won't you? But maybe it'll backfire on them yet. The girl who wanted to be them was clear about what she liked best about Charlie's Angels. "Well – they're women and they beat men."

Ruth Wallsgrove

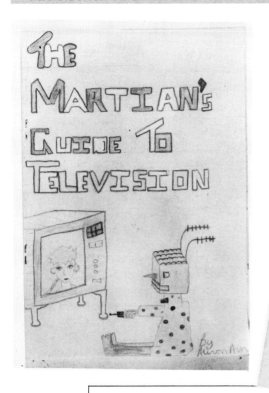

T.V. — WHAT TO WATCH FOR MARTIANS

There are programmes and there are programmes. Here I am reviewing the two extremes – the quite reasonable and the terribly awful. These are the ones you will probably enjoy most or least as the case may be, though the latter is more likely.

EASTENDERS : Tuesdays and Thursdays 7.30pm BBC1. This is actually quite good, giving an interesting view of the inhabitants of London's poorer sector. They seem incredibly unlucky, with an amazing number of problems. The Eastenders' lives are centred around a 'pub', where they drink "alcohol" mixed with various liquids pleasurable to the tastebuds.

STAR TREK : Thursdays 6:00 pm BBC 2
A disgraceful programme portraying Vulcans as humans with plastic ears. They are in fact green blobs of plasma as everyone knows. Imagine us Martians joining a federation run by humans! A primitive spaceship rushes about the galaxy killing any aliens in its path. Definitely not one for the kids.

MUSIC   great cover!   ...out BBC 1
This is great, I laughed ... ... through it. These earthlings are so stupid – I could answer before he'd asked the questions.

SPORT : Any time, any place, anywhere.
When sport is on I turn off. All it is is teams of humans trying to beat other teams of humans. The object is to get this ball into the other teams' goal/net/hole.

FILMS : Randomly placed, all channels.
Films are like programmes only much longer. You can watch without being left in suspense until next week.

COMEDY : It isn't a programme.
Humour is a difficult concept for Martians to understand. You wouldn't be expected to comprehend the subject on your first or even second visit. Humour is indicated by a strange gurgling, coughing sound in the background, particularly when humans fall off, or into, things. Most of the time you know what's going to happen, but earthlings still gurgle anyway.

STEPHEN SPENCER 4HY.

/ Alien reviews by students **Alison Ain**, top left, **David Bardwell**, top right, and **Stephen Spencer**, above

Now you try writing a review in one of the following ways:

Either: Choose a programme you have recently seen and write a review of it for your school magazine. If you do this in a group, watch the programme using individual viewing journals and then discuss your reactions together before writing.

Or: Write the script of an interview in which you are the guest. The host asks you to imagine you are stranded on a desert island for one year. You can take with you five television programmes. Which programmes would you choose and why? In the interview, the host questions you about the reasons for your choice.

Or: You are a Martian visiting Britain. Write a review of this week's viewing for the folks back home.

Or: You are asked to select the ten Best Ever Programmes to show during a television festival. You have to choose the best ever comedy programme, the best ever documentary, the best ever children's programme and so on. Write down your choices and prepare an article for the *TV Times* or the *Radio Times* explaining what you looked for in making your choice, and why these particular programmes deserved to win.

TELETEXT REVIEWS ON *ORACLE*

Viewers' reviews appear each day on Oracle, the teletext service which appears on ITV and Channel 4 if you have a television set adapted to receive it. Teletext allows written information such as news headlines, weather reports and programme information to appear on screen. There is an equivalent service on BBC called Ceefax. Pages of information are called up by dialling the number on a remote control device. If you have a teletext set in school or college, browse through pages of Oracle and Ceefax. Look up today's reviews this way:

- Turn the television to the ITV channel.
- Press your remote control 'TEXT' button and wait for the 'menu' to appear.
- Call up number 223 on the remote control and wait a few moments until the RSVPtv page appears.

The RSVPtv service is part of the group of pages called TV PLUS which is all about television programmes. Prepare a review of a recent programme for RSVPtv in one of three ways:

- by writing a guest review no longer than 100 words to the address given below about one recent programme, including the name, channel and date of the programme, as well as your own 'out of 10' rating. If your review is used at the weekend, you receive a free full colour souvenir print-out. Here are two reviews which have appeared on screen recently:

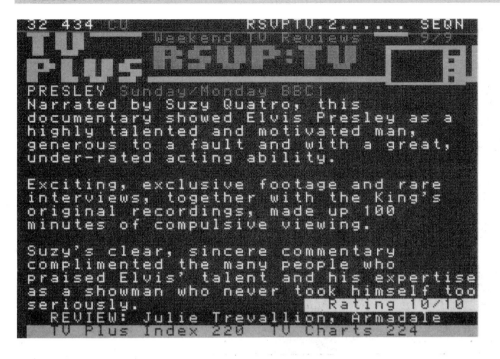

```
32 434 CU            RSVPTU.2...... SEQN
            Weekend TV Reviews        9/9
TV PLUS RSVP:TV
PRESLEY Sunday/Monday BBC1
Narrated by Suzy Quatro, this
documentary showed Elvis Presley as a
highly talented and motivated man,
generous to a fault and with a great,
under-rated acting ability.

Exciting, exclusive footage and rare
interviews, together with the King's
original recordings, made up 100
minutes of compulsive viewing.

Suzy's clear, sincere commentary
complimented the many people who
praised Elvis' talent and his expertise
as a showman who never took himself too
seriously.                  Rating 10/10
   REVIEW: Julie Trevallion, Armadale
TV Plus Index 220  TV Charts 224
```

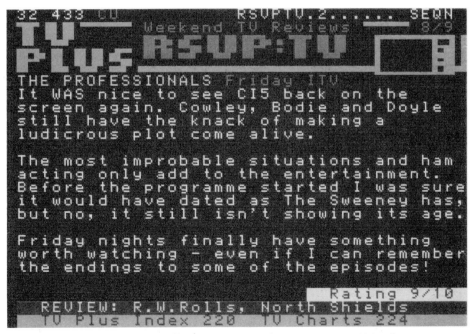

```
32 433 CU            RSVPTU.2...... SEQN
            Weekend TV Reviews        8/9
TV PLUS RSVP:TV
THE PROFESSIONALS Friday ITV
It WAS nice to see CI5 back on the
screen again. Cowley, Bodie and Doyle
still have the knack of making a
ludicrous plot come alive.

The most improbable situations and ham
acting only add to the entertainment.
Before the programme started I was sure
it would have dated as The Sweeney has,
but no, it still isn't showing its age.

Friday nights finally have something
worth watching - even if I can remember
the endings to some of the episodes!

                            Rating 9/10
   REVIEW: R.W.Rolls, North Shields
TV Plus Index 220  TV Charts 224
```

– by letter to RSVPtv, ORACLE, 25–32 Marshal Street, London WIV 1LL. There is a £10 prize for the best letter of the week.

– by phone on 01 734 7672 leaving a recorded message.

REVIEW PROGRAMMES

A number of programmes review the week's television and deal with viewers' opinions. List the ones you know.

In groups, set up a studio discussion about programmes you have watched this week. Record this discussion 'live' onto a video or an audio tape.
Afterwards, discuss the following questions:

- What were your feelings about your own performance?
- What effect did the discussion have on your opinions?
- Did the presence of the video or tape recorder make any difference to you? Do you suppose it makes a difference to people appearing on television?
- Who chose which programmes to review? Who do you suppose chooses them for television review programmes?

Critics on television often seem confident and slick. But then, they are experienced and their performance has been edited to look good. It is healthy and right to change opinions as you talk: that is the point of discussion. One of the important things to remember about television is that it makes people sound more definite than they actually are. Viewers feel amateur by comparison, and think that television is for experts and professionals. This is perhaps one reason why the opinions of viewers are not often aired.

Now devise a further programme based on viewers' opinions, and ask other people in the class to contribute to it. Consider including:

- viewers' letters
- studio discussion
- statements made on video
- reviews
- round-up of the week's viewing
- cross-questioning programme-makers

Perform this programme 'live' in the classroom or record it in sections onto video. Either way, you should experience some of the pressures and problems of dealing fairly with viewers' comments.

Afterwards . . .

Discuss the effect of different formats. Does a letter, for example, have a different effect from a personal appearance? Are formal reviews more limiting than studio discussions?

Audience

HOW WE WATCH

In groups, discuss the following points:

1 In your household, who decides which programmes to watch? How do you resolve the problem of wanting to watch different programmes?

2 Estimate how many hours of television you watched over the last week, and write down the number. Now list the programmes you have watched and work out the number of hours precisely. Discuss the results.

3 What are your pet likes and dislikes about television?

4 Do you have a favourite channel and why?

5 What other things do you do while you are watching television?

6 Do you have a video recorder and if so what use do you make of it?

Someone in the group should take notes to share with the rest of the class later.

Now think more closely about the way television is used in your own home. Tonight, or as soon as possible, keep a secret diary as you observe the other people in your home watching the television. Notice what else they do during the programmes . . .

> e.g. Do they talk during programmes?
> Do they talk about the programmes?
> Do they react to the programmes in other ways? How?
> How much attention do they give to programmes? How do you know?
> Do they watch programmes to the end?
> Do they ever switch off, change channels, fall asleep?
> Do they ever leave the room? When? Why?

Do you do any of these things? This is quite an important question, because many people believe that television influences the way we behave. You have probably heard the argument that violence on television encourages violence on the street, or that young people will imitate their heroes by trying dangerous stunts. Is it true that we sit and take in everything that television throws at us? Politicians certainly think it influences voters, and try to use it in their election campaigns. Advertisers invest huge sums of money in television commercials – they know it will be worth it.. But is anyone really taken in by everything they see? Are you? Were your family 'under the influence' when you observed them? How do you rate the power of television?

CLASSROOM SURVEY

You will need a list of last night's programmes for this exercise. Conduct a survey of the whole class to find out:

1 How many hours of television each person watched last night.

2 Which programmes were watched – only count the programme if the person had it on for at least half its length.

Illustrate your results with bar charts like this:

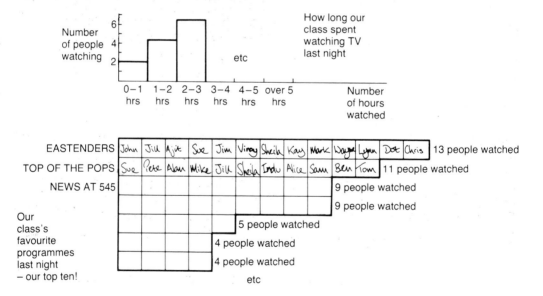

Afterwards, write down your thoughts about the results. Did they surprise you or were they predictable?

    Would you expect the results to be different if you asked a group of adults? Try it. Ask as many adults as you can to help you do the survey again. What do you find? People do not always watch the programmes you would expect. Other than personal preference, what factors influence the number and type of programmes watched?

ADVERTISING

The ITV companies are particularly keen to collect information about their audiences because they depend on the money which advertisers will pay for airtime. The cost of this airtime varies depending on the size of audience so there are constant surveys to find out how many people watch particular programmes and what type of people they are. An advertiser might pay a huge sum to put on a commercial at the 'right time', instead of paying less to be fitted in at the convenience of the company.

Here is a typical weekday's viewing from an advertiser's point of view:

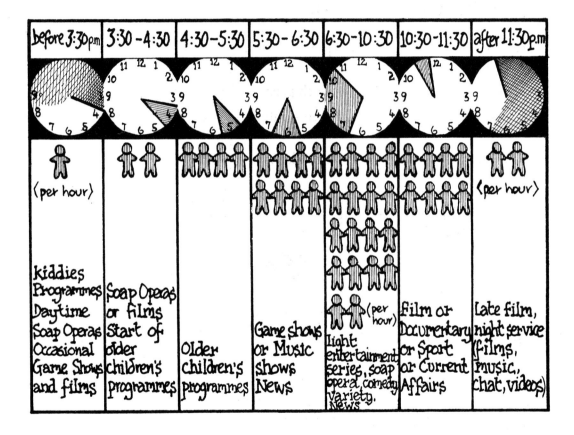

before 3:30pm	3:30 – 4:30	4:30 – 5:30	5:30 – 6:30	6:30 – 10:30	10:30 – 11:30	after 11:30p.m
(per hour)						(per hour)
kiddies Programmes Daytime Soap Operas Occasional Game Shows and films	Soap Operas or films Start of older children's programmes	Older children's programmes	Game shows or Music shows News	light entertainment series, soap opera, comedy, variety, News (per hour)	film or Documentary or Sport or Current Affairs	Late film, night service (films, music, chat, videos)

You can see in each time slot the type of programmes and the relative size of the audience watching at that time.

When would you expect to see advertisements placed by the following advertisers?

Bright Eyes Instant Coffee – extra strong coffee
Lula-Belle – the crying, walking, sleeping, talking doll
New LP Offer: Smoochin' – your favourite slow dance tracks
Yupimoto Sports Car – for young executives
The Sunday Slush – a new Sunday newspaper full of news, star gossip, great pix

Buccaneer Radio – a new pop radio station: non-stop music
Wideacres Fun Park – fun for all the family: zoo, amusements, etc.
Suncruise – cruises down the Nile at new low prices

Name at least *five* things an advertiser will consider before placing an advertisement on television.

Look ahead to tomorrow's television schedules. Predict the sort of advertisements which will appear at:

   8.30 am
  10.30 am
   1.00 pm
   4.30 pm
   7.00 pm
  10.30 pm

Watch or record them and consider the following questions:

1 How accurate were your predictions?

2 Working backwards from the range of advertisements, can you work out the type of audience which is expected?

3 Can you spot any advertisement which has been specially placed in its spot because of a particular programme next to it?

4 Watch and listen to the break between programmes and the advertisements. What do you notice? Why is such a particular effort made to mark the transition?

SCHEDULES

How do the stations decide what programmes to make, and when to screen them? It depends a great deal on the money available and the need to put on programmes which will be varied and popular. A close eye is also kept on the other three channels who are competing for the attention of the audience. Room for manoeuvre is limited. **Jane Larner** explains how schedules are compiled:

What do you take into account in scheduling a programme?
The most important consideration, really, is the time of day. It sounds obvious but you have to start from the available audience. We employ market researchers to analyse who is watching and when. They produce a weekly book of their findings which are studied in detail by our own research department. Our schedule starts at 5.15 pm on Friday when our audience includes many children and old people. We aim programmes at them because they are the available audience at that time of day, but as the evening goes on we have to cater more for the housewives and working men who join the audience. By 9 pm we assume an adult audience. After 10.30 pm, programmes will be aimed more at a young male audience; they tend to stay up later.

There's no such thing as an ideal schedule: you make the strongest one you can with the available material, and try to guess what the opposition will do. The aim is to make the most of the material you have – to support weak programmes by placing them between popular ones, to put strong programmes in the most competitive slots and also to dent the opposition by drawing attention away from their most attractive programmes.

Another factor is balance: we try to provide a range of programmes. People would soon get bored with a constant diet of drama, drama and more drama. So we offer a variety of programmes. At the moment one thing we are lacking is strong situation comedy – ideally we'd like three or four good comedies in our schedules.

What do you schedule against a popular established programme on another channel?
Well, against something like *Top of the Pops*, we look first of all at who isn't watching, and provide a programme to appeal to them. At other times, we have to compete head on for the audience by offering our own popular entertainment. On Saturday evenings, we schedule our strong programmes – *The A-Team* and *Blind Date* – to overlap BBC's popular opener *The Late Late Breakfast Show*.

Do viewers stick with the channel they start watching?
Maybe not as much as they used to, but if you get them at say 7 pm, 50 per cent of them will probably stay with you. You try to hook them for the evening – if the next programme looks good, they'll stick with the channel, so you sandwich the weaker programmes between the stronger ones. That can work for a half-hour programme but not usually for a longer one.

How does ITV's scheduling system differ from that of the BBC?
Both BBC1 and BBC2 are scheduled by a single controller who is able to show complementary programmes which will not compete for the same audience. ITV and Channel 4, by contrast, create their schedules separately. We meet to establish common programme starting times where possible, but the arrangement isn't binding.

Within ITV, the schedule is currently agreed by the 'Big Five' companies – Thames, LWT, Granada, Central and Yorkshire – whose controllers and planners meet to present their forthcoming programmes to the network and to draft the next season's schedule. The 'Big Five' companies make most of the programmes but do select from those made by the other ten ITV companies – the 'Regionals'. Discussions are in progress to give these regional stations more opportunities to have their programmes networked.

Jane Larner, Forward Planning Manager, LWT

On pp. 112–115 there are full schedules for a weekday and a Saturday during August. Like all weeks, these schedules have their special features such as the coverage of an important political party conference and a major athletics event. You will see that certain programmes have been deleted. Discuss what kinds of programme would be suitable for these slots. Take note of:

- the length of programme required
- the time of transmission
- the likely audience
- the competition on the other channels
- programmes which come before and after

TUESDAY

BBC 1

06.00	Pages from Ceefax
06.35	Edgar Kennedy (film)
06.55	Weather
07.00	Breakfast Time
08.55	News
09.05	Children's BBC (children's programmes)
10.00	News
10.05	**A**
10.25	Children's BBC (children's programmes)
11.00	News
11.05	Athletics
12.00	News
12.05	Dallas (soap opera)
12.55	News
13.25	Neighbours (soap opera)
13.50	Putting Women in the Picture (documentary)
14.40	Athletics
18.00	**B**
19.00	No Place Like Home (situation comedy)
19.30	**C**
20.00	Juliet Bravo (cop series)
20.50	Points of View (viewers' letters)
21.00	News
21.30	Screenstory (historical drama)
22.40	Athletics
23.40	Weather

ITV

6.00	**D**
9.25	News
9.30	Stingray (children's programme)
10.00	The Coral Island (children's drama)
10.30	University Challenge (game show)
11.00	Alfie Atkins (children's drama)
11.10	Rainbow (children's programme)
11.25	News
11.30	About Britain (magazine series)
12.00	The Sullivans (soap opera)
12.30	News
13.00	The Woman in Question (film)
15.00	Arthur C. Clarke's World of Strange Powers (popular interest series)
15.25	News
15.30	The Young Doctors (soap opera)
16.00	Children's ITV (children's programmes)
17.10	Athletics
17.45	News
18.20	Athletics
18.40	The Roxy (pop music)
19.10	**E**
19.40	Another Side of London (documentary)
20.05	**F**
22.00	News
22.30	First Tuesday (documentary)
23.30	Athletics
24.00	Exit Dead End (film)
01.40	Nashville Swing (country music)
02.30	News
02.35	Three's Company (situation comedy)
03.00	Probe (film)
05.00	Donahue (popular interest series)

TUESDAY

BBC 2

06.55	**G**
07.20	(Close down)
09.00	Pages from Ceefax
09.20	Conference Report (current affairs)
12.30	Pages from Ceefax
13.20	Pigeon Street (children's programme)
13.35	Pages from Ceefax
14.00	News
14.02	Conference Report (current affairs)
16.05	News
16.10	**H**
18.00	Athletics
19.05	100 Great Sporting Moments
19.20	Tricks of the Trade (special interest)
19.50	Floyd on France (cookery)
20.30	Brass Tacks (debate)
21.00	Who? (film)
22.30	**I**
23.20	Weather
23.30	Open University

CHANNEL 4

14.25	Say It With Flowers (film)
15.45	Valued Opinion (special interest)
16.00	A Full Life (documentary)
16.30	The Gong Show (game show)
17.00	Bewitched (situation comedy)
17.30	The Pocket Money Programme (popular interest)
18.00	Conference Report (current affairs)
18.30	World Alive: Spain (natural history)
19.00	**J**
19.50	Comment (personal opinion)
20.00	**K**
20.30	The Great Trailer Show (excerpts from film)
21.00	**L**
22.50	Michael Jackson in Bad (drama)
23.20	Hoarded Dreams (jazz music)

SATURDAY

BBC 2

14.20	Network East (Asian magazine)
15.00	No Limits (pop music)
16.05	**G**
17.55	Athletics
19.20	**H**
20.00	Dennis O'Neill (music)
20.40	Top Crown (bowling)
21.25	Stage Door (film)
22.55	**I**

CHANNEL 4

9.30	Listening Eye (magazine programme for the deaf)
10.00	The Home Service (programme about homes)
10.30	**J**
11.00	Same Difference (programme for the deaf)
11.30	Dancin' Days (drama series)
12.30	Sea War (documentary)
13.00	Monsieur Hulot's Holiday (film)
14.40	Pardon My Berth Marks (short film)
15.00	Horse Racing
17.05	Brookside (soap opera)
18.00	Right To Reply (viewers' responses)
18.30	Ourselves and Other Animals (natural history series)
19.00	**K**
19.05	Beyond Belief (religious programme)
19.30	No Easy Walk (documentary series)
20.30	All Muck And Magic (gardening)
21.00	A Profile of Arthur J. Mason (drama)
21.45	The Table (short film)
22.00	St Elsewhere (soap opera)
22.45	**L**
23.55	The Spiral Staircase (film)
01.30	Night Has A Thousand Eyes (film)

SATURDAY

BBC 1

8.30	The Family Ness (children's programme)
9.00	Dogtanian & The Three Muskehounds (children's programme)
10.55	**A**
11.05	Elephant Boy (film)
12.30	Grandstand (sport)
17.55	News
18.10	**B**
18.45	Carry On Screaming (film)
20.20	**C**
21.10	Bluebell (drama)
22.00	News
22.15	Athletics and Boxing
00.30	Starsky & Hutch (cop series)

ITV

7.30	TV-am
9.25	**D**
11.30	The Roxy (pop music)
12.00	Wrestling
12.30	Athletics
13.00	News
13.05	Saint & Greavsie (sport)
13.30	The London Connection (film)
15.00	Darby O'Gill and the Little People (film)
16.45	Sports Results
17.00	News
17.05	**E**
18.30	Happy Anniversary 007 – 25 years of James Bond
19.30	**F**
20.00	Summertime Holiday Special (variety)
21.00	News
21.15	Crazy Like A Fox: The Movie (film)
22.45	News
22.50	Athletics
23.30	Lust In The Dust (film)
01.00	Night Network (night service)

You will find the actual scheduled programmes below to compare.

    – Were you surprised by any of the answers?
    – Did you find some answers easier to get than others? Can you explain this?
    – Do you notice any differences in the scheduling policy of each channel?

Do not assume that the schedulers got it right – some programmes do flop. There is no such thing as the perfect schedule, because demands are always changing. Even the controllers who compile the schedules have to compromise. The need to draw big audiences, and therefore big advertising money, often competes with demands for specialist programmes with small audiences or 'quality' programmes which are expensive to make. In other words, a lot of decisions come down to money rather than principle, practicalities rather than preference.

Scheduled Weekday Programmes

A Neighbours (soap opera)
B News
C EastEnders (soap opera)
D TV-am
E Emmerdale Farm (soap opera)
F Pretorius (cop show)
G Open University
H Children's BBC (children's programmes)
I Newsnight (current affairs)
J News
K Brookside (soap opera)
L Special People (film)

Scheduled Saturday Programmes

A Cartoons
B Krankies' Elektronic Komik (comedy/variety)
C Seaside Special (variety)
D Get Fresh (children's programme)
E The A-Team (action series)
F Family Fortunes (game show)
G The Swan (film)
H Newsview
I The Devil Rides Out (film)
J Scotland's Story (history)
K News
L Australian Football

Watchdog

INTRODUCTION

What happens if television broadcasts something which hurts or offends its viewers? What if people don't like a programme for any reason? Can they do anything about it?

1 First of all, think of common complaints which people make about television. You have probably seen programmes in which viewers are able to voice their criticisms, and you also know that thousands of letters are written every year to complain about programmes and to praise them.

   What kind of things do people complain about? Make a list.
   e.g. bad language

2 Secondly, what can a viewer with a complaint do about it? Make a list.
   e.g. turn off the television

3 Thirdly, think of your own recent viewing. Is there anything which struck you as unfair, objectionable, one-sided, tasteless, or downright boring? Discuss examples among yourselves, and consider what action you feel able to take and why.

THE IBA

The IBA – Independent Broadcasting Authority – controls the transmitting stations, selects the ITV companies and lays down rules about what can be broadcast on independent television and when. The BBC is overlooked by its own governors whilst the IBA currently keeps an eye on ITV and Channel 4 to see that they keep to the rules. For example:

- Nothing should be broadcast which will offend against 'good taste and decency'.
- Nothing should be broadcast which will encourage crime.
- News and politics should be presented with 'due accuracy and impartiality'.
- Advertising should be kept quite separate from the programmes.
- Only seven minutes per hour may be taken up with advertising.

One of the jobs of the IBA is to consider the complaints made by viewers and to act on them if it agrees that a television company has broken the rules. It can make the company apologise or change its programmes, and every few years it can take away its right to broadcast (the *franchise*) and give it to someone else.

   Television is watched by millions of people who may be influenced by what they see. Is this a bad thing or a good thing? Is it even true that people are so easily influenced? It is hard to know for sure how much we take in without realising it. Do you think *you* are influenced by the things you see and hear on TV?

DISCUSSION

Bearing in mind some of the problems raised so far, imagine you are a member of a committee dealing with viewers' complaints. You may find it useful to split your group into viewers, programme makers and independent committee members, so that several views are represented.

Viewers' telephone calls are recorded in a log book kept by the duty officer, and it is the job of the committee to:

(a) Consider the accuracy and fairness of each call.
(b) Discuss what further information it needs (if any) to reach a decision.
(c) Decide what it ought to do about the complaint.
(d) Keep a record of the discussion, and a special note of any decisions taken.

Read the following material carefully and then discuss it as a committee.

PROGRAMME SCHEDULE FOR THAT DAY

7.00   Breakfast Time Show

9.00   News

9.30   Cartoons (all popular American titles)

10.30 Children's programmes – puppet show
                              – school quiz
                              – painting workshop
                              – storytime (Goldilocks)

12.00 Lunch Time Show – fashion, interviews, music

1.00   News

1.30   Educational programmes – History (Elizabeth 1)
                              Geography (Lake District)
                              English (Shakespeare)

2.30   Cookery programme – vegetarian starters

3.00   Today's Play – about moving home

4.00   Teen Show – pop music, interviews, film extracts

5.00   Quiz

5.30   The Bad Boys – regular drama about a gang of unemployed teenage boys

6.00   News, weather and sport

6.30   Midway Programme – local news, views and issues

7.00   Talk My Way – regular comedy about teaching English to foreign tourists

7.30   Heartbreak – soap opera about the lives and loves of the immensely rich family of Lord
        Delaney

8.00   Blaster – American cop programme

9.00   Memory Lane – looks this week at the final months of the First World War

9.30   Laughter Lines – quickfire comedy from the regular team

10.00   News

10.30   The Big Movie: favourite American cowboy film

12.00   Prayertime: The Bishop of Midway prays for world peace

EXTRACT FROM THE DUTY OFFICER'S LOG

5.00   *Annie Smith, 315 High Street, Bordertown*
        Teenager – half-term – found the day's programmes boring – nothing for her age group.
        Should do more for teenagers, especially during school holidays.

6.05   *Mrs I. Braithwaite, 7 Primrose Terrace, Wittington*
        Swearing in *The Bad Boys*. Counted nine examples of 'extreme bad language'. Unnecessary.
        Unpleasant image of young people. Encourages foul language. Most offensive, especially at
        this time of day.

7.05   *F. Lang, 2 Pelham Place, Bancroft*
        Political bias on the Midway Programme. Fifteen minutes given to interview of local
        Conservative councillor, whereas only four minutes were given to the Labour Party. Also
        notes that two other local parties were completely unrepresented. Election this year – should
        give equal airtime. Intends to write to IBA.

7.30   *P. de Bruxelles, Charteris School, Wittington*
        Foreign language student – offended by view of foreigners expressed in *Talk My Way*. Objects
        to the way foreigners are shown as foolish and ridiculous. Found the jokes tasteless, and the
        characters stereotyped. Especially disgusted by the words used by the teacher to describe
        the students.

9.15   *Irene Granger, Lapis House, Boxwater*
        Disturbed by degree of violence – four murders already this evening. Obsession with death –
        programmes about war (*Memory Lane*), murder investigations (*Blaster*), street crime (*The
        Bad Boys*) and even violence in the news. Particularly disturbed by news pictures of bomb
        victims. Feels that the mugging scene in *The Bad Boys* might encourage youngsters to go out
        and do the same.

9.35   *Geraldine Gaston, Gill Street, Ingledown*
       Disturbed by intolerant attitude towards other nationalities:
       – anti-Irish jokes in *Laughter Lines*
       – stereotyped foreigners in *Talk My Way*
       – reviving anti-German feeling in *Memory Lane*
       – lack of programmes about other countries and cultures
       Considers the range and tone of programmes to be racist.

9.40   *Margaret Treadwell, 142 Bassett Road, Wittington*
       Annoyed by insulting sexist stereotypes displayed in *Laughter Lines* – nearly all male
       comedians, same old tired mother-in-law jokes. Rest of evening's viewing equally
       male-dominated – *Bad Boys* (no Bad Girls?) – American cops predictably male, too. *Memory
       Lane* – men at war. Even prayers said by a man.

9.45   *Mrs P. Hodge, 42, Warner Close, Ingledown*
       Feels that as a senior citizen, living alone with little entertainment beyond her television set,
       the station does not screen enough programmes for her age group. Enjoyed *Heartbreak* but
       not much else. Can we do more programmes to interest the elderly, please?

10.30 *Lee Smith, 23 Bradford Road, Linstone*
       Too many American programmes – why can't we make our own?

10.45 *Margaret Walker, 5 Linton Terrace, Boxwater*
       News depressing – all death, doom and disaster. Why not show some good news for once?

When you have finished your discussions you may like to consider these questions:

   – What problems do the IBA and BBC face in deciding whether a complaint is
     justified?
   – Why do so few people bother to make complaints?
   – Why should TV companies change programmes which offend a few, but please a
     lot of people?

Think Tank

INTRODUCTION

A think tank is a group of people who are paid to produce and consider new ideas. In this exercise you are to imagine yourself as a member of a think tank for a television station. First of all read through the agenda below and jot down any ideas which spring to mind immediately. Secondly, get into small groups and share ideas. Work through the agenda and prepare a short report on the main points of the discussion as well as a list of recommendations.

Item 1: Night Service

The station has decided to offer an all night service and wants the think tank to give some thought to the following points:

- Who will the night audience be?
- Will they watch at night in the same way as they do in the day?
- What kind of programmes will they want?
- Are there any kinds of programme which would be entirely unsuitable, and why?
- Which advertisers might be eager to screen night commercials?
- Suggest a typical night's viewing between the hours of 11 pm–7 am.

Item 2: Agony Aunt Programme

A recent survey has revealed that many people are fascinated by problem pages in magazines and newspapers. It has been suggested that the station might produce its own version of the problem page on television.
   The think tank has been asked to:

- consider how this might be achieved. What form would the programme take, and who would be in it?
- come up with more ideas for programmes adapted from magazines and similar reading matter.

Item 3: Equal Rights

The station wishes to improve its policy on sexism and racism. It has resolved to:

- put an end to sexist and racist attitudes in its programmes.

– employ an equal number of men and women as presenters.
– increase the number of presenters from ethnic minorities to reflect their numbers in society.
– encourage open discussion of these issues on television.

How easy will it be to implement this policy? As a practical test, make a close study of today's viewing schedule and report back on the extent of the problem and how the station might begin tackling it.

You will need a copy of the *Radio Times* or *TV Times* for detailed programme information about one station.

Item 4: Research

The station is aware of the growing number of people who have their own satellite dishes to receive television from other countries and tune in to the new international channels. There is a children's satellite channel, for example, and one which shows bestselling programmes in English. Money is made by selling airtime to advertisers.

The company wants the think tank to research:

– who is watching satellite television
– which advertisers use it
– if it affects your own station

What you have to consider now is how to find this information quickly, cheaply and accurately.

From experience, the think tank knows that collecting such information is not easy, and you can never be quite sure how accurate the results are. A brief discussion might suggest the probable answers, but how can you be sure you are right?

Discuss the possible ways of researching this information and make a list of options, noting the advantages and drawbacks of each method. Decide which method you will use and why.

Tempting Offers

INTRODUCTION

The moving image on the television screen is compulsive: it holds attention because it is bright, flickering and ever-changing. Each cut signals a new and different picture; the viewer can hardly resist looking up to see what is there.

Television pictures are luminous and fizzy compared with the subtle soft tones of film in the cinema. They are transmitted to your home as a constant stream of electrical impulses, which your television set reassembles into pictures. Each one is made up of hundreds of tiny lines – 625 in the UK system – and each line is 'updated' in turn 25 times a second. In this way, small changes are brought to the screen very quickly, so that the picture seems to change quite naturally. In fact, what we are seeing is a still picture being rapidly updated, so that there is an illusion of movement.

DRAWING IN THE VIEWER

We trust our televisions and feel comfortable with them. They are like one of the family, perched in the familiar corner of the living room. The terrible events of the news are at a safe distance, out there somewhere in the world beyond the screen, and the nightly gunshots seem snugly familiar. Television insulates us from the cutting edge of personal experience, often welcome after a hard day's work.

Because television pictures look like the world as we see it, we sometimes make the mistake of thinking of it as a simple 'window'. But it is not. The pictures have been selected, sounds have been added, and we cannot see beyond the square frame the camera has chosen. Someone else has chosen and ordered the world we see on the screen. In doing so, they have chosen for us where we should see it from. For example, the camera which points upwards to the actor makes us look up to her, too. If a camera shows a surgeon leaning overhead, we are put in the position of patient. If on the other hand, we see both surgeon and patient across the operating theatre, we feel like onlookers. In this way, television decides for us where we stand both physically and emotionally.

Turn on the television and consider the picture which appears. Where does it place you, the viewer, in relation to the centre of the action? Try this with all four channels. In each case, decide why the viewer has been placed in a particular spot.

The pictures are also loaded in the way they use lighting, background, make-up and so on. Dim lighting and soft music will encourage us to look on with romantic expectations; harsh make-up and lighting may lead us to view a character as severe; sinister music will cause us to treat a character with suspicion. The way a story is told will persuade us to build up sympathy with particular characters. If we follow the fate of one person through the programme, then we can't resist seeing things from their perspective.

Judge the distance and the angle of the camera, when you next see one of the following on television:

(a) a newscaster
(b) a contestant on a game show
(c) a pop star

What do you notice?

Notice the background scenery the next time one of the following appears on television:

(a) a scientist
(b) a trade unionist
(c) an expert
(d) the Prime Minister

What do the backgrounds suggest?

Because television is so suggestive, because it makes us be the viewer it intends, we must keep a check on its effects. This is particularly important in areas where public opinion is changing. For example, many programmes speak to viewers as men. Sports commentaries are often guilty of this. They call sportswomen 'girls' but sportsmen are 'men', and they sometimes take a very patronising attitude. Similarly, programmes often assume we are all white, including history programmes which speak of 'our' history as that of Olde England. These small but persistent assumptions can be insidious: women and black people, for example, soon learn to think of themselves as insignificant viewers, almost watching someone else's television service.

Listen to five minutes of an athletics programme with both men's and women's events. Do you notice any difference in the way the male and female contestants are described?

ADVERTISEMENTS

So television makes a direct appeal to the eye and mind, and positions the viewer conveniently. Advertisers make good use of this to draw attention to their products. Viewers experience a sense of need which they will remember next time they are out shopping.

Advertisements are captivating because they are so brief and intense. Some tell a mini-story in which you, the viewer, fill in the details in your imagination, particularly about the effects of the products. If you feel involved in making sense of an advertisement, you will identify with the product. The chances are, you will buy it because deep down you feel stimulated, flattered and hopeful of its promises.

Most of all, advertisements make promises – nothing specific, just a promise of well-being and a better life if you have that product.

Think of advertisements which make a secret promise that if you buy the product you will acquire:

(a) excitement
(b) self-confidence
(c) fun
(d) power
(e) sex appeal

Do the opposite: watch several advertisements and study the promises they make.

Advertisements offer us dreams of a better future. It is hard to imagine an advertisement which is completely honest and informative. Oddly enough, we respond well to the reassurances of promises and dreams.

Making your own advertisement is an interesting moral exercise because you have to draw a line between promises and honesty.

Choose one of these products:

(a) a chocolate bar
(b) a new book
(c) a luxury shower foam

Design a package or cover for the product which will set its image, and prepare a storyboard for a fitting television commercial.

The one on p. 126 was drawn by student **Alison Cram**:

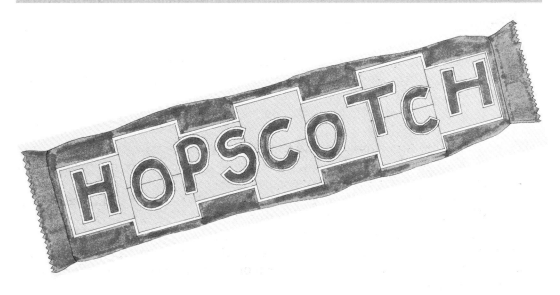

H = Happy feeling

O = Original, new taste

P = Packed full of goodies

S = Sweet surprises when you bite

C = Creamy chocolately taste

O = Orange centre

T = Tasty, tangy flavour

C = Chewiness

H = Handy size

...the new, fun, tasty chocolate bar.

ALISON CRAM

Afterwards . . .

Make a list of the things you do *not* say about your product – its price, look, effectiveness, quality, availability, durability, size and so on . . . and justify your reasons for leaving them out.

We can never see the whole truth on the screen. We can only guess what has been left out. What lies beyond the square frame? What happened just before? What happened just after? What information have we not been given?

We can't expect to see things from every angle. We have to accept the angle we are given. We put our trust in programme-makers whose outlook on life shapes our own. This is neither a conspiracy nor a clumsy piece of bias: it is simply part of the process by which programmes are made. For this reason, it is important that every one of us knows how programmes are made and reflects on them to become more intelligent and discerning viewers.